Searching in Circles

Searching in Circles

Poems by

Rose Anna Higashi

© 2025 Rose Anna Higashi. All rights reserved.
This material may not be reproduced in any form, published,
reprinted, recorded, performed, broadcast,
rewritten or redistributed without
the explicit permission of Rose Anna Higashi.
All such actions are strictly prohibited by law.

Cover design by Shay Culligan
Cover image Melancholy by
Odilon Redon French (1840–1916),
courtesy of Unsplash
Author photo by Wayne Higashi

ISBN: 979-8-90146-800-5
Library of Congress Control Number: 2026902409

Kelsay Books
502 South 1040 East, A-119
American Fork, Utah 84003
Kelsaybooks.com

*This book is dedicated to
the memory of my son David

and to my nieces and nephews
Peter and Kathleen
Michael and Matthew
Shana and Diana
Patrick*

*May each find something of value
in these pages.*

Acknowledgments

Some of the poems in this collection have not been published previously. Others have appeared in various books, publications and journals. Some of the haiku which appear in "Circling the World with Haiku" were published on the website *myteaplanner.com*, by Rose Anna Higashi and Kathleen Pedulla, or in the blog "Tea and Travels," by Rose Anna Higashi, which appears on this website.

Thank you to the following publications, in which versions of these poems previously appeared:

The Agape Review: "Tide Pooling"

Blue Wings: One Woman's Guided Flight Toward Healing, (Paulist Press, 1995): "At the Mission," "The Shepherd," "Winter Dawn" (originally titled "Birthday")

The Ekphrastic Review: "Hildegard's World," "The Peanut King," "Dream Girl," "Radiance"

myteaplanner.com: "Siblings," "Kin," "The Myth of a Thousand Pies," "Sonnet Counterpoint," "Tide Pooling," "Margaret in May"

Poets Online: "Uncle Dick's Funeral," "Sleeves," "Eleanor of Aquitaine Reflects on the Wildfire at Big Sur," "August Back Then," "Barbie and Ken's Divorce," "Planning a Spring Reunion," "Turning Pages," "Elegy for Auntie: A Triversen," "A Beginner's Guide to Baking Cakes," "Shifting," "Waiting in the Waves" "Ala Moana Park," "The Grace of Ghosts"

Rose Anna's Gift, (1979): "The Saint" (originally titled "The Hero"), "The New Year," "Magic," "Satori," "Winter: The Survivor," "An Irish American Meets Herself" (originally titled "An Irish American Meets Himself"), "Patriotism"

Thresholds: Literature-Based Composition by J. Sterling Warner, (Harcourt Brace College Publishers, 1997): "The Gambler's Lover in the Rat Pack Days" (originally titled "Thoughts of the Gambler's Lover")

Contents

I. THE ELDERS

Haley's Comet Returns: 1986	17
The Myth of a Thousand Pies	18
Out in the Ozarks, Looking for Black Jack Springs	20
Fourth of July	22
For Dad, an Elegy	25
Mom Fell Down	26
Uncle Dick's Funeral	28

II. HERALDS AND HELPERS

The Shepherd	33
Guanyin	34
Hildegard's World: The Secret of the Rose Window	35
Mary	37
Teresa Takes Off Her Shoes	38
Summer's Moment: In Memory of Matsuo Basho	40
Circling	41
Emily at the Oven	42
Gerard's Journey to Joplin	44
Beyond the Dream	45
The Peanut King	46
Radiance	48
Coming Again	49
Thank You, Claude	50
The River	52
Carl Jung Responds to a Student's Comment at the University of Zurich	53

III. MYTH, MYSTERY AND MEMORY

Satori	57
The New Year	58
Strength	59
The Saint	60
The Dancer	61
Sleeves	62
Magic	64
Treasure Fire	66
Egypt	67
Tide Pooling	68
Stones	70
Winter: The Survivor	72
Waiting in the Waves	74

IV. THE WAYS OF WOMEN

A Tanka for Murasaki Shikibu, Author of *The Tale of Genji,* the World's First Novel	77
Lady Kasa Writes Even More Poems to Otomo Yakamochi	78
Eleanor of Aquitaine Reflects on the Wildfire at Big Sur	80
Dorothy Wordsworth Vents in Blank Verse	82
Black and White	85
Elizabeth Barrett Browning in Florence	86
Queen Liliuokalani's Farewell	89
A Sonnetish Valentine	92
Dream Girl	93
The Gambler's Lover in the Rat Pack Days	95
Gracie in the Sixties	96

Greta in the Eighties	98
Seeing Him	99
Betrayal	100
Barbie and Ken's Divorce	103
Joan on the Mower	104
Deep Blue	106

V. PLACES AND PEOPLE

Tucson	109
August Back Then	110
Mt. McKinley	112
At the Mission	114
Californians	115
Mexico	117
Borobudur	118
Costa Comes Home	120
Osaka Castle: Summer Solstice	122
Planning a Spring Reunion	124
Ala Moana Park	126
Circling the World with Haiku	128
Life on the Island	138

VI. BACK AT THE BEGINNING

Siblings	143
The War Kids	144
Patriotism	146
Thank You, Peter	148

A Valentine Tanka	150
A Beginner's Guide to Baking Cakes	151
August Birthdays	153
Kin	154
A Tanka Trio	155
Winter Dawn	156
Turning Pages	157
Orchids	158
An Irish American Meets Herself	159
Shifting	160
Time	162
Elegy for Auntie: *A Triversen*	163
Remembering Rwanda	164
Dear Rose Anna: The Poet Celebrates Herself	166
The Grace of Ghosts	168
Sonnet Counterpoint	169

I.
THE ELDERS

Haley's Comet Returns: 1986

Grandma saw the Comet back in 1910.
"I was still in high school back then," she tells us,
While she braids her rug.
"We went out into the cornfields
And looked at it through smoked glass."
"Why the smoked glass?" I ask her.
She isn't exactly sure.
Her fingers keep the three strands going
Out from the center.
She has to keep it on a card table now
The circles have gotten so large.
We have tickets to the observatory,
But even so, the city lights will get in the way.
"They was a real nice tail to it.
I could see it real good."
The strips of old stockings shift
From taupe to tan to a rosy cream;
Some of them are left over
From when she was young.
Some I brought this evening
In a paper bag.
"They don't expect it to be as bright
This time around," I tell her.
"But at least I have to try for a glimpse."
"You go on without me," says Grandma.
"I can't see that far anymore,
And besides, I've got this rug to braid."

The Myth of a Thousand Pies

Grandma told me the story,
And Mother told me too.
How many times in childhood did I hear
About Great-grandpa and the pumpkin pie?
Sometimes it was a long tale,
And sometimes short.
What triggered it?
Talk of pies probably—
> Blackberry cobblers in August on a picnic table in the park
> Custard pie with fresh cream in spring
> Apple pie in autumn when the Ozarks turned to glory
> And pumpkin pie at harvest time too—
> Round and golden brown like the moon.

"Your great-grandpa, Nicholas Roberts,
Used to eat a whole pumpkin pie at lunchtime.
Great grandma would carry it out to the field in a dinner bucket,
And he'd fold it over like a sandwich
Right there in the hay,
And eat it standing up."
Sometimes the standing up part seemed significant.
At other times it was the fact
That he folded the pie in two.
But eating a whole pie was always the marvel.

I've seen an old photograph of him
Standing in the yard of the wooden house in Arkansas
That he built by himself.
There he was in his high starched collar
And his droopy moustache, upright like a ramrod, tall and slim.
Yes, slim, this man who could eat a whole pie at once,
In even less than a single sitting, since he didn't sit down.
With the last bite, he picked up his pitchfork
And kept on bailing the hay.

Out in the Ozarks, Looking for Black Jack Springs

Grandma says they had a rainy winter,
And even last night, my first night home in a long, long time,
There was the sharp sound of water on the metal awnings
Above the sleeping porch windows
As I lay looking out at the big elm
Against the cloudy night sky. Lightning flashed,
And the little red bud tree came out of darkness.
Then the thunder. The neighbors' puppy howled and hid
Under the back porch steps, over across the alley.

Today, we're out in the country looking for the old cemetery
Where some of our people are buried.
Grandma thinks she knows. "Is it Oak Hill or Quaker Valley?
No, that's not right. They put your uncle Jimmy over there.
Maybe it was over to Joplin or out to Lowell."
Grandpa's ninety and he's driving, but he shouldn't be.
He's veered into a lot of ditches lately, so I've been told.
Grandma said, "You might as well shoot him
As tell him he can't drive."

A bob-white quail skitters across the road;
Grandma points out a scissor-tail flycatcher, then a cardinal.
Grandpa's elderly Oldsmobile wanders over to the left,

Across the faint center line. No one is coming from the other way,
So I stay silent and focus on the wild roses, jumbled like weeds
Along the old fences as we lurch over toward Shoal Creek.
It's higher than usual, and the mad tangle of vegetation
Grows right down to the water's edge,
And some of the trumpet vines dangle in.
Tiger lilies are everywhere, and a few white-faced cattle
Graze right up to the dense thickets of sumac and oak.

The road sort of peters out, and they forget about the graveyard.
Grandpa tells me they used to drive his Model T
Over to Black Jack Springs, somewhere around here,
And fill up their barrels with spring water.
Grandma tries to tell me just how good
That spring water tasted.

Fourth of July

Around sundown, we gather on the front porch—
Grandma and Grandpa, Mother, Dad and me.
I'm too grown up for fireworks,
But since we're here for the holidays, Dad and I decide
To shoot a few. We light the punk
And throw the firecrackers, big loud Black Cats,
Out onto the sidewalk. They pop, and their innards
Of rolled newsprint scatter across the gray cement.

Grandpa can barely hear the loud explosions;
Instead, his eyes are up in the catalpa tree.
Through the leaves, he sees the streetlight
Down on the corner come on. "Comes on every night
At nine," he tells us. "The one on the corner
Beyond that, just a little later. And the last one,
Two blocks down, two minutes after that.
The second one will be coming on directly."
And he's right. We see it light up quietly,
A soft orchid glow a block away.

Dad and I get bored with the firecrackers
And decide to shoot off the whole string all at once.
I lay it out on the sidewalk, touch the punk
To the wick and scramble back to the porch.
The sparks and pops and paper bits
Go on for the longest time.
Mom and Grandma don't appreciate the noise.
Grandpa, calm as he can be, keeps watching
For that last streetlight, down at the end.
Sure enough, it comes on too, right after
The last Black Cat goes off.

Time for sparklers now. I take a whole box
And poke them into the front yard grass.
As I squat down, I can see the sky off to the west
And north has turned a warm orange,
And Venus is bright silver above the sunset.
I set off the sparklers; they hiss and sizzle,
Raining down a lovely shower of stars
Into the humid lawn.
Grandpa looks up above the treetops.
There's a star that he likes to watch for.
He doesn't know its name, but
It comes out after the streetlights,
And it shines so much brighter than the
Constellations. The sparklers leave a stinky smoke
That settles over the grass and spent fireworks,
But Dad and I have saved the best—
Three fountains—a Silver King, a Whistler
And a Golden Willow.
The light from the west reflects off the
Aluminum window frames
Of the neighbors' house across the street,
Making a pinkish copper glow.
I set the Whistler on the sidewalk and light it.
Grandpa doesn't hear. The sparkles shoot out in beautiful curves.
Mom and Grandma say they've never seen anything prettier.
The Silver King and Golden Willow go last.
From where I sit on the porch swing, I want
Those lovely gentle sparks to go on forever,
Setting off the twilight with tiny comets—
A glittering little Milky Way in our front yard.
After the fountains, we have nothing left

But the glow from the sunset
Reflected now from clouds, strangely
Shaped in lines ascending from the neighbors' roof.
"Them's Jacob's Ladder clouds," says Grandpa.
And they do look like rungs, tinted
Pink and gold. I remember the song
From Sunday school, "We are climbing Jacob's ladder. . . ."
Grandpa must have sung it too.
To the south, I see his star before he does
And point it out to him.
His eyes are still sharp. They follow
My finger into the sky, and he smiles
When he spots it. He gets up now to go in
And put his pajamas on. He doesn't like to go to bed
Until he's seen that star.

For Dad, an Elegy

The rains began the day of your death,
And the piper, gritty as a highlander,
Stood in the drizzle
To pipe your coffin into the grave.

Now you rest beneath a pepper tree
Safe in the sweet damp earth.
I will miss the way you loved to look at trees,
The way you noticed shades of gray
In the winter sky.
You would have marveled at today's mist
And the bright blossoms
Just being born among the deep
Azalea leaves.

Mom Fell Down

"Of course she fell," said the nosey neighbor
Across the street. "Isn't she in her late eighties?
Everybody falls if they get that old."
What do you know? I thought.
But I kept my mouth shut.
It was sudden, though.
She was just standing in her own driveway—
And fell over.
Four bones in the shoulder broken,
A cracked pelvis.

"We may need to do a complete
Shoulder reconstruction," says the surgeon,
Bored and looking past me,
The uninteresting middle-aged daughter.
He looks like he spends two hours a day
Attached to an exercise machine
Lined up in an upscale gym
With two dozen other success cases
Staring out a plate-glass window
As they tread, tread, tread
To new age sounds on their iPods.

He's the hot shot with the knife.
And after it's all over,
Still bored but smirking slightly,

He tells me that he was able to do it all
With four pins.
He's just that good.

"Of course, it won't really matter in her life,"
He comments, just before dismissing me.
"She can't remember anything anyway."
What do you know? I thought.

Mom Fell Down, P.S.

Martin, the boy who grew up next door,
Came to her rescue.
He's middle aged now, with a truck
And a receding hairline.
He was over at his dad's house
Drinking beer in the front yard after work.
He heard her calling across the ditch.
"Help! Help! Help!"
She trusted, and help came: Martin her hero.
He didn't have an iPod in his ear.

Uncle Dick's Funeral

I had nine uncles, and now all of them are dead.
I didn't know any of them well, but I heard stories
About my dad's brothers, what a bunch of wild Irishmen
They were, moonshiners and party boys, whose tales
Are still being embellished by their grandsons, old men now,
Sitting on the bench at the fire house in the little Kansas
Town where they all grew up.
My mother's younger brother, Uncle Dick,
Was nothing like them. He was quiet and reserved,
Stunningly handsome, yet he didn't seem to know
That he was. He had a wife who worshipped him,
But he hid from her most of the time in his basement
To be with his true loves, music and books.
He taught junior high band and choir during the day
And composed choral music at night. On the rare occasions
When I heard him sing, his mellow baritone voice sounded
Like the opera records I had heard. When one of his sons
Mangled his hand in a lawnmower,
Uncle Dick was sick with grief for weeks.
My mother told me he hated violence and was a
Conscientious Objector during the War,
But he served in the army as a chaplain's assistant,
Playing a portable organ for services on the battlefields.

I was about ten when I learned this news, and I thought
About it by myself for a long time. I concluded that
He must have been very brave to refuse to kill anyone,
Even our enemies, when all the other patriots were
Enlisting for combat and probably calling him a
Coward. I didn't see Uncle Dick often in my childhood, but
He was the only uncle who took the time to talk to me,
His youngest niece, and he loaned me
One of his books once. He lived to be an old man
And was my last uncle to die.

The singer at his funeral wasn't in Uncle Dick's league,
But to my surprise, it was a military service, with flags,
And trumpets and real soldiers in uniform,
Carrying his casket. Then an officer stood up
And told this fantastical tale about Richard,
Rushing around in the Battle of the Bulge without
A weapon, pulling wounded soldiers from both sides
To safety, earning a fabulous medal for valor.
Is he talking about my uncle?
I wondered. Why didn't anyone in the family
Ever tell me this story?
Were they still ashamed of his cowardice?

II.
HERALDS AND HELPERS

The Shepherd

It was rocky on the hillside where David sat
Under an orange sapling in the hot noon.
The sheep grazed in silence;
Some knelt to rest beneath the silvery leaves
Of three olive trees.
The smallest lamb came to rest at David's feet.
He placed his long fingers in her cloudy wool
And felt her holy heart.

He thought of his father
And his handsome brothers
Gone to the temple without him.
Here he was, an equal to sheep.
He looked up through the glossy leaves
Toward the heavy sky.
A golden orange was centered
Between his eyes and the sun.
They are the same size, he noticed,
An orange and the mighty circle of light
The other tribes worshipped.
David turned his gaze to the sacred eastern hills
And lifted his harp in his ripe hands.

Guanyin

Guanyin holds her rosary of rock crystal,
And her gaze is as calm
As the deep roots of the Bo tree
Where the Great Buddha sat in stillness
Waiting for grace.
Her breath is the east wind at dawn,
The serene breeze that will never cease.
At her feet a pair of Mandarin ducks
Nestle at rest.
The petals of the lotus hold all three,
The Queen and her feathered servants,
Together in a river of gold.
They will wing through our dreams,
Calling us to compassion.

Hildegard's World:
The Secret of the Rose Window

Precious Hildegard, when you entered this world,
A magic millennium was also being born.
Greece's glory had faded.
Centuries of thinkers disappeared after explaining
Beauty, truth, rhetoric, and the different kinds of love.
The Romans were gone too, leaving their solid bridges,
Aqueducts and the old church in Bamberg behind,
Along with their stodgy marble gods, resembling only themselves.
Your world, Hildegard,
Was filled with upward-flowing light,
With angels everywhere, soaring on deep lapis blue wings,
Their haloes aglow, through the realm of dreams,
Visions, miracles, symbols and saints.
Demons, dragons, beasts, serpents, and wolves inhabited this
Stratosphere, along with the secret sounds germinating in the
Black Forest where the elves
And the fairies lived. And all were real, as real as bridges,
As authentic as thoughts.
But the greatest beings in your world
Were Mary, emerged from the shadows,
Now wrapped in her blue mantle, as she
Ruled the sky and the sea sitting beside
Her shining, golden son.
Hildegard, you belonged in this new reality,
You and your music, your responsories, played on the psaltery at
Mass, your fragrant garden, filled with blue rosemary and healing,
Greening herbs.
You lived in this swirling circle of color,
Where the chant of women's voices lifted like bells,

Linked together in a dancing daisy chain
Of yellow light, pink and crimson light, claiming dawn and dusk,
The green light of fragrant mountain pines
And summer chestnut leaves.
Your world was Mary's world, the place where stones
Were transformed into towers,
Into spires that aspired to reach the circle
Where the cloud of witnesses surrounded
The very throne of God.
Under the towers and turrets of these new temples
Of sacred stone,
The rose windows, built in your lifetime,
Carried light from the farthest star
Into the darkest crypt, casting the demons into obscurity.
And even now, after a thousand years, no darkness can overcome
A rose window's light.

Mary

> *How but in custom and in ceremony*
> *Are innocence and beauty born?*
> —William Butler Yeats, "A Prayer for My Daughter"

This is her year,
This year and every other,
Until in custom and in ceremony
Innocence and beauty are reborn.
In Lent when the first leaves begin to bud,
Like pale green beads in oak fingers,
Her breath quickens,
Her mantle lifts in the west wind
And spreads over stone walls, crumbling
Over battlegrounds,
Turning in the kindness of time
To mossy places where wild doves feed
With the brave jays and the timid finches.
She inhales the fragrance of the early plum,
Feels the warmth of every candle lighted in piety,
Hears the tinkle of each rosary,
Gathers the prayers and guides them
To the feet of the Peace King.

Teresa Takes Off Her Shoes

Juanito prays at night
When thousands of stars
Fill the summer sky
And holy Earth is still warm
From the long hot days of Castillo.
He sits out there in the darkness
With all the night creatures
And surrenders to the Spirit
While I in my cloister
Wander from room to room,
Motionless in my long, sweet,
Delicious hours of prayer.
We are on the same journey, he and I,
As the Lord has placed us both in Avila,
This remote and ancient place
In the high rocky countryside.
There is no time here.
Yes, the church bells ring,
And we can hear the bleating of sheep
On the distant hillsides, marking the intervals
Of dawn and twilight,
But we do not count the hours.
We count nothing—

Not the stars or the crickets,
Not the words that others wish to speak to us.
We give ourselves to the fragrant breath of the Spirit
In our ears, on our skin, deep,
Deep in the castles of our hearts.
It is the castles and nothing else that we count
As we ready ourselves for the labor God has assigned.
We have kneeled down to wash each other's feet,
Cleansed our own hands,
And now, nearly alone, we must travel throughout
España and clean the sacred Houses of God.

Summer's Moment:
In Memory of Matsuo Basho

The days of fog and deep bone chill
Evaporate like a withered moor
In a troubling dream.
In summer we are wide awake,
And daylight strolls beside us
Through the luscious long gloaming
And into the sacred firefly time.
Luminous gold fills our eyes,
And the warm air wraps itself
Intimately around us.
We walk with the posture
Of a snow-free pine,
Our limbs lifting upward, light, buoyant,
And June's jay, with his laughing voice
And his lake-blue plumage,
Flutters just ahead.
The day will come to meditate
On a crow and a leafless tree;
But not today, in summer's moment.

Circling

The birds build their nests in circles
Because theirs is the same religion as ours.
                                  —Black Elk

I am blessed with a round window in my kitchen.
I can wash my hands at the sink
And look, as through a telescope,
At the shifting leaves of the oak,
The bright oleanders, turning in the summer wind,
The long feather-fingers of the eucalyptus.
The red-headed woodpeckers,
Strong searchers, find their food in the dark branches,
Feed their children high in the deep green,
And the circle of sky holds us all.

Emily at the Oven

Lavinia says I must not wear White Lace
When I am making Gingerbread.
It's horrid laundering linen
With molasses stains, she says.

Her knuckles turned red as Embers
Scraping on the washboard,
But I say she vanquished the spots,
So how was Heaven harmed?

Out to the Henhouse then down to the Cellar
For the Sorghum and the priceless Spice.
My flour barrel runneth over.
I will escort the weevils out.

White lace and Gingerbread—
Can she not see the Partnership?
Like puffy clouds behind the Dogwood
Or the black Cat napping near the milk Pail.

And when it is time to launch it—
Smelling like a ship from India—
But really, just across the Graveyard
To the house where the sick woman lives—

Nothing but the sky-blue tea Towel will do
To wrap the fragrant Cake.
But I know Lavinia's schemes—
Like a plunder Pirate, she loves her sundering:

Replace my blue beauty, the one with the Violets
My own hand engendered,
And wrap my little Sacrifice in the shabby one
Cut from a flour sack and hemmed in hasty Stiches!

More prudent, she will say, Prune person that she is—
In case they forget to return it
When the old lady dies.
Prudence—that should have been her Name.

She knows nothing of the glory of White Lace
On a jonquil morning
Or Violets wrapping a Gingerbread
In their sweet Embrace.

Gerard's Journey to Joplin

In this dramatic monologue in the form of an expanded and counterpointed Italian sonnet, the British Victorian Jesuit poet, Gerard Manley Hopkins, inadvertently finds himself in Joplin, Missouri, Gateway to the Ozarks and birthplace of the American poets, Langston Hughes and Rose Anna Higashi.

Oh, the wonder of it! Even the names
Of the little pubs are a glory-journey!
Wendy's—puffing my spirit up in cumulous-curious,
Zephyring the scent of potatoes over
The vast mystic highway. Macdonald's—calling
Clans and thoughts of plaids red and russeter
Than the dark dawn over Hadrian's Wall,
Recalling pipes like angel-hawks squawking
Out God's muster in picnic-places and
Refectories. There too is Grace in August's inferno,
The air itself a baptism in the bath of God.
There is a moisture I have never imagined,
And even in empty lots where the walkways crack
With the up-pushing roots of elms, there is life.

    And more life—vines and mosses, mimosa sprouts
    And catalpa beans, dangling like the fingers of Christ.
    In sagging roofs and crumbling brick, the Spirit

    Her very self weighs down with an instress
    So stimulating than even the cats seem caught in prayer—
    How can the humans help but be holy?

Beyond the Dream

On the days when the pine groves stand hazy,
And the sea lanes draw back . . .
No, life is not all misery
Here by the sea lanes.
   —Kanze Kiyotsugu Kunami, *Matsukaze (Wind in the Pines)*

I drive down the mountain
And the straight, strong pines
Start to mingle with the little maples—
Maples whose three-pointed leaves
Have started to turn,
The color of Oklahoma clay,
The color of brick homes in Oklahoma.
It is never sudden.
The pines continue well down the hillside,
But the vision of that first bright leaf
Among the shadowy needles—
The intimacy of it moves me,
As though winter slipped backward
Into autumn.
I remember the blue laces on Basho's shoes;
In his eyes they were iris.
Now, the strong gust at the height of a pine
Becomes my husband's breath,
A windfall three hours before dawn.
And even this morning,
The sunrise in late September
Almost smelled like gingerbread;
The rosy lights on the Christmas pine
Almost stretched across the eastern sky.

The Peanut King

On a painting by George Washington Carver

I know this place. I've been here. Diamond Missouri.
It's just a few miles from Joplin, where I was born.
Straight east, then south on Highway 59, though
The road probably wasn't there in your day.
It looks like you painted this picture in winter,
Just at twilight, or maybe dawn. The walnut trees look almost
Bare, and that might be a little frost on the ground,
Though I don't see any smoke coming out of your cabin, which is
Gone now. That big space in the back must be your garden.
And those trees, just in front of the distant horizon could
Be pines or white oaks.
This is the Ozarks, an ancient magical land of rocks
And cliffs older than humans, rivers and underground springs,
Deep cold caves meandering under the earth, darker inside
Than a starless night.
Those of us who were born here
Carry the Ozarks in our hearts forever.
But there was always an elephant in the room,
Although we didn't use that expression in those days.
Everybody used the S words, forming an invisible,
Curving line, like a serpent:
Slavery, Segregation, Separate, but equal.
All the children knew that was a lie.
We could hear the sorrowful Gospel music
Coming out of the old unpainted church right across the street
From Grandma's church.
We could see the shabby schools and
Broken down cabins like yours.
But the grownups all believed the lie,
Except for just a few, like my mommy.

She's the one who told me about you,
A former slave who transformed American farming and made
Missouri famous. You were Missouri's diamond,
The Peanut King.
You grew peanuts in your garden, performed experiments
On them, and invented all kinds of wonderful new things
To make life better for the sharecroppers and everybody else.
Mommy had a list in her head of all your accomplishments, like
Crop rotation, whatever that was.
I was a little girl who loved peanut butter and jelly sandwiches,
So you became my hero.
I think you were Mommy's hero too, because
She wanted to make something of herself even though her family
Didn't have much. And she did.
She and my daddy got out of the Ozarks before us kids started
Believing the lie.
And she earned herself a doctor's degree.
There were Ozark men besides you who came along later and
Did well for themselves,
Harry Truman, Langston Hughes and Johnny Cash,
But you were smarter than they were.
You went off to Tuskegee and became a professor, a scientist,
Always helping. Now a garden fills the space
Where your rickety old cabin used to be.
Now your old homestead is a National Monument
With an African American woman park ranger.
Now kids learn about you in nice clean schools.
I can't honestly tell you that old serpentine line
Has disappeared, but you were the sunrise
That drove some of those snakes back in the cave.

Radiance

Camille! Everyone should call you Uncle!
You were a gift giver, a mentor, a lifter of hearts,
Starting in your balmy childhood in St. Thomas.
Born into brightness, surrounded by tall palms,
Shifting shades in the warm, slow rivers, inching
Toward the soft sea, women chatting on the shore,
A parasol reflecting the sun's eternal radiance,
You saw everything and needed to paint each holy
Moment—shadows, colors, every one of them,
And darkness, where every shade of green and brown,
Red and blue still linger along with light, which
Is never extinguished.
You were the herald, crowning the peasants,
The farmers and their humble homes with glory.
Your jewels were the knots on trees,
Clods of dirt, the ragged clothing of children
And the drooping leaves of the olive trees in the
Last silvery shades of dusk.
Of course, you came to the City of Lights,
And on the *Boulevard Montmartre a Paris*
You still saw it all. In your old age, you painted this vibrant
Street six times, looking down from a high hotel window
When your eyes had started to fade. You still discerned
The daylight, the boundless joy of Mardi Gras, cloudy
Mornings, winter, spring and finally, night.
Nine electric streetlights formed a line to the
End of vision, and all along the way, light and darkness
Danced in endless exuberance with the faint dots of stars.

Coming Again

for William Butler Yeats

A rough beast can be a priestess in disguise,
A journeyer through the tired landscape
Sent from the inner eye of vision
To the place where water pools
Bluer than Mary's veil,
And birds in their dignity
Soar to the highest place
And cast their scarlet feathers
Like sacred seeds on a summer breeze
For a harvest so long awaited.

Thank You, Claude

Thank you, Claude, for getting up before dawn,
Year after year, painting the waterlilies in winter's
Cold, summer's insects, and spring's hesitation
Before the huge pink blossoms emerged from
The sedge and the mud under your Japanese bridge.
You never stopped. With your palette in your aging hands,
Your brush kept moving until every twilight
Sank into the starry darkness.
You listened to the birdsong,
To the sounds of your children playing
On the other side of the pond,
Smelled the ratatouille from your own garden
Your wife cooked with butter and herbs
In your sunny yellow kitchen.
And when night came to your simple farmhouse,
You gazed at the Japanese prints on the walls,
Thought about tomorrow—clouds or rain
Before sunrise? Pale yellow light at noon?
A pink glow on the beech tree and the bridge mingling
With the waterlilies and the peonies at dusk?

There were days when you boarded a boat
Down the Seine to Rouen to view the
Ancient Cathedral, as precious as waterlilies
To your discerning eyes. Like the water
And the blossoms, the old Cathedral shifted
With the seasons and the light.
Because of you, the spires still sparkle in sun and rain
For the world to see, and your waterlilies are everywhere.
This little poem, paltry compared to your paintings,
Is my humble offering of gratitude.

> *At the Ohara Museum of Art, Japan:*
>   Claude's waterlilies
>   Hang in Kurashiki. Swans
>   Glide past the stone bridge

The River

I remember back in Idaho
Decades ago, my daddy
Would sit on the front porch in the evening,
Smoking a cigarette,
And listening to the Snake River.
We couldn't see it from our house,
But he knew it was there.
Now, as I sit on the back steps,
Thinking of him,
I watch the tide grow higher,
See the stacks of clouds on the horizon
Turn pink, layer by layer,
And listen to the endless call of the sea.
I can't hear him,
But I know he's here.

Carl Jung Responds to a Student's Comment at the University of Zurich

How can I tell you not to travel that road?
I went there, along with every other elder who survived,
Though so many of us never came back.
That Irishman was one of those—
You know him.
He lived here in Zurich, and wrote a book so brilliant
That no one could understand it.
And that sad British woman, Frau Woolf,
Clever though they were,
Their art added up to nothing
Because they lost their way in the maze
And forgot their Alpha and Omega.
They were no match for the giants—
Herr Doctor Faustus of Heidelberg and Jesu,
Who both walked in the murky desert
And dialogued with the devil.
You are at the University.
No doubt you have learned
How those epic encounters ended.
And do you see yourself as their equal?
Have you looked into the black eyes of death?
If not, how will you resist the delicious myth
That everything is yours?

I know how the dark side glitters.
I was young and handsome once, gorgeous
And able like Icarus to soar to the sun.
I know the world circles the young,
Hangs golden baubles over you

And crowns you with dazzling stones,
Gives you presents for your pockets, as it did for me,
And sparkling chariots to race and run.
Everyone worships the young,
And they trick you
Into worshipping yourself.
The invisible elders know all this,
Though few listen to us,
And I can see in your mocking eyes
That you are dismissing me.
But my eyes are no longer ravished
By the shimmer of the world,
And I have learned along with the other old ones
Through ridicule, defeat and shame,
But also through the quiet joys—
      Morning sunrise falling through a peacock's feathers
      The sacred glow of every roseate twilight
      The sweet whisper at the entrance to the cave—
That we are not the rulers
Of the universe.

III.
MYTH, MYSTERY AND MEMORY

Satori

Enlightenment comes
They say,
Like a knife in the inner ear
Changing balance
Stabbing sounds into stillness
Like lilacs crashing
Through snow

The New Year

The winter solstice rolls by
And the lean time comes
When the tree turns brittle
And drops its needles,
The rice cakes begin to grow mold
And every last relative, too
Has turned away.
January, then, with its cold, feastless days
Presents itself—
Unavoidable.
And everywhere
Gray branches
Rake the gray sky.
Can't we,
Like tea brewed from snow,
Steep
And grow green?

Strength

Reflecting on a tarot card

Somewhere between the two points
Of the pelvis bone. That's where the lion lives.
He is everything they say he is.

The size of his paws alone could awe you,
And the sinews that circle up his shoulders
Are heavy from running for the taste of blood
Like the lover whose last thrust
Sends the feathers soaring into the sky.
His teeth are honed for the weighty
Haunches of a buffalo and the strong neck
Of a zebra. Height and hard hooves
Only make him lunge farther.

Hold his jaws lovingly in your sacred hands;
Touch the yellow tendrils of his mane.
Let him live in your abdomen
As in the tall grass at twilight.
He will serve you all your life.

The Saint

Dolphins, they say, can talk to their mates,
And whales, too, murmur through the strong salt,
Sensing needs, speaking perhaps of the past.
Maybe they imagine their calves
Swimming through the blue waters of the moon.
But do they whisper when the storms start them sorrowing,
Of a hanged whale, harpooned in the heart,
Her pulse engulfing the ocean itself—
Beating on, waning, waxing, lapping the edges
Of eternity? Have they given her a name?
And in speaking of her, do their own whale-hearts heal?

The Dancer

He's always been there—
Kicked in the corner at Christmas
When you're busy baking that Yule Log
And steaming the Plum Pudding in the big pot.
Then there's the New Year;
Everybody has to watch the playoffs
And eat their black-eyed peas.
The dancer shivers outside on the patio
With his nose pressed to the glass.
Only the dog licks his trembling fingers
And sidles up to his lithe legs.
The same cold pine tree
Reflects in their eyes
And the same winter hawk
Darkens their shoulders
With his long wing.

When every gingerbread man's head
Has been bitten off, and the Niners
Have lost again, you finally
Toss the dancer a sidelong glance
And open the door a crack.
That night you take a slow, hot bath
And rub your body with oil,
Knowing he will forgive you.
And sure enough, you awaken
At the blackest moment of the night;
His slender fingers are tangled in your hair,
His strong legs wrap around you,
And without a word, the dance
Resumes.

Sleeves

When the mornin' comes and it's time for me to leave
Don't worry 'bout me; I got a wild card up my sleeve.
—Susanna Clark and Carlene Carter, *Easy from Now On*

Emmylou sings these lines like a trickster—
Like that wild German, Emil Nolde,
Turning his back on the Blue Riders
With just a paintbrush between his fingers,
Like Jesus, stumbling off among the stones
On the edge of a crossover,
Without even a crust of bread
Or a pocket to put a windfall into.
But at least
He had sleeves.

Trickster—
You'll meet him or her again
On some other threshold,
Maybe as the worker whose job it is
To put the steering wheels on Teslas,
But who instead calls in sick
To stay home and play with his baby—
The student who cuts her botany class
And is seen sitting on a hillside
Writing haiku in a field of rocks
And wild lupine—

Or the painter who can't face another lecture
On brush stroke technique, perspective
Or how to mix the perfect shade
Of cobalt blue.

Picasso himself could return
To teach this lesson,
And our trickster would wander
Into his own back yard
To stare at the stains on his neighbor's fence.

If he sits until midnight,
The sky will turn strange and wild
As few have seen it, even in dreams.
And when he has taken it in,
He will stumble out among the stars
Filling his sleeves with color and light.

In China they have one word which means
Either blue or green.

Magic

We lost it somewhere—
Maybe before Tutankhamen's brain
Was pulled through his nostrils with a silver
Hook and placed in its own gold holder
Shaped in the form of the magic boy.
Something got in the way—
Parameters were put up
And some supposed that magic could never
Lead us out of the tomb.

What was it?
The image of a man hanging head down—
His smiling gaze set straight for the horizon?
Or a simple sunrise shining like a garnet
Into green Druid eyes—eyes that saw between stones,
Read signs beyond the sky?

How could such prizes have been dropped
In the water, or lost in containers,
Put into caves? Now we look down,
Standing in the darkness with nothing but numbers
On our hands. Not a single emerald warms the palm.
Clean to the edge, we shake when the wind passes us by
And don't even know why it blows.

We hold this heavy air in our fingers
While claiming that our hands are free.

Still somehow we lean toward the sun's glitter
And the feel of real jewels on our flesh.
The time for grasping rises up again
At the place where the dawn first fell on us
The place where the wind begins.

Treasure Fire

They say it hovers just above the ground,
A fire, ruby colored,
Flickering in the north wind,
Burning hot and steady
Even when the rain falls cold and warlike
In the winter solstice.
They look for it in green places
Near the holly, near the hemlock
And the ash groves.
Sometimes it even dances
Over mossy stones.
Old men speak of it in whispers
On starless nights.
Sometimes a child will tell her grandmother
Of a fire she saw from her window
Flaming out like the wide wings
Of the snow goose.

Men have searched their whole lives
For the Treasure Fire,
The light that marks the crevice
Where the jewels lie buried
Deep in earth's secret womb.
Men have killed and lied,
Plotted and dreamed for the Treasure Fire.

The old women know this;
They sit by the hearth
As the storms grow colder.
They have seen the Treasure Fire
Everywhere it burns.

Egypt

I think of your fingertips—
The dark side of a late harvest peach.
I think about the veins
That flow down the backs of your arms.
We don't have rivers here,
But I float down the Nile in those arms,
Eating apricots,
Letting the sun that shown
On Isis and Osiris
Take us as far as there is to go.
We laugh with the jackals on the riverbanks,
And the mud and cutting rushes at the edge
Never stop us. We are washed clean.
And as we enter the dark sunset
Hanging over the water
Like a martyr's hushed breath,
We never turn our eyes behind us.

Tide Pooling

There is nothing here, you say—
Nothing to look at,
Just a sort of brown and soggy place
Here by the dunes—
Uneven rocks, hard to climb on,
Bumpy under your soles.
Then this nothing little pool
Stranded by the tide
Stuck in the sand and smelling salty.
Nevertheless, you crouch,
Wobbling a little, and peer in.
Nothing. You were right—
Except, what is that anyway?
Oh, not that but those—
Are they little fishes?
Lots of them, small brown beings
Darting into dark corners.
And what?
Those feathery things,
Swaying as the tide laps lightly—
Sea urchins? Anemone?
Marine worms?
There are thousands of them on every rock
Waving to one another—Or is it to you?

You stare amazed, and then you spot him—
The hermit crab, sidling sideways
With someone else's shell atop him.
He makes his way past coral shrimp
With their striped arms.
How could you have failed to see
Those vibrant red beacons
Flashing in the shadows?
Are you the kind who would miss the angels
Shouting in the sky?

Stones

There are roads with so many stones.
Sharp, metallic cinders wait by the side
Of the simplest path.
Even those whose lives are filled
With the innocent drone of radios,
Or bees in the backyard,
People who hope for nothing more
Than a bargain at the grocery store,
Dream less than their dogs,
Even these find themselves cutting their feet,
Stumbling over unknowns
Cluttering up the way.

Yet there are other rocks
Whose edges have worn smooth,
Rocks that are firm to step on,
Cool to the fingers,
The color of dawn when held to the light.
Looked into, these have the same strange harmony
As the dark thing
At the center of a rose,
As the echoes whispering forever
Through the old ridges of a cowrie shell.

A dog will pick up a pebble
And carry it in his mouth;
A child will keep one until he is ninety
In a secret place.

Winter: The Survivor

The black tree's thin limbs,
Fragile as starving deer,
Scrape the gray sky,
As though begging gold
From the cold silver sun.
Green is an unworded memory,
And the rabbit, colorless with cold,
Stands motionless, gazing unfed
Toward the edge.
The green-necked wild duck has gone,
And the only sound
Is the groan of stones.

And into this cold continuum,
She strides, purple velvet hung from her limbs,
Crushing snow with her feet laced in leather.
Humbling the horizon with her stare,
She sings across the cold
An ancient song.
The torch in her hand assaults the ice;
Her pockets hang heavy with apples,
Green and red, and her skin, like fruit,
Grows warm, the only jewel
In the white and black world.

The places where she has stepped
Collapse in gray hollows as she stalks on
Toward the sun.
The sound of her singing rings after her,
Touching the black branches.

Her hot aroma spreads over the snow
And long after she is gone,
The rabbit stands thawed,
Having seen the survivor.

Waiting in the Waves

Dawn and dusk are soundless
When, like the first pink peony opening,
A glow appears at the murky line
Between sky and sea,
And later in silence,
The huge red orb descends,
Surrounded by quiet islands,
In the dark Sea of Japan.

Doves coo before sunrise.
On the windward coast,
Mynahs call out at first light,
And the waves lap and lilt on the sand
Or crash against the lava stones
If high tide comes with twilight.

But light itself and darkness speak only to the soul—
To the listeners who lift our hearts and eyes,
Breathless, grateful
For the gift that will come.

IV.
THE WAYS OF WOMEN

A Tanka for Murasaki Shikibu, Author of
The Tale of Genji, the World's First Novel

I see you alone,
Across the Bridge of Dreams through
Cherry blossoms, leaves,
Gently falling snow. I see
Tears as your hand lifts the brush.

Lady Kasa Writes Even More Poems to Otomo Yakamochi

(Nara, between 710 and 784)

A Choka

After days of endless heat,
Suddenly the twilight breeze
Lifts the oleanders
And the blossoms dance
Like the women at *obon*.
You, my distant lover,
Hiding in summer heat,
Come and lift me from the stillness
Of these endless summer nights.

How I envy
The deep pink oleanders
Light as laughter
Tall as a man on horseback.

Ride your tall horse
Through the twilight
Feel the summer wind in his mane
Think of me
Sleepless beneath the oleanders,
Dark and restless.

A Haiku

Summer's yellow rose
Withers on the bush, like an
Old woman near death.

A Tanka

Now old and near death,
I lie all night in the moonlight.
Sleepless, I wonder
Why my children stay away.
Was I the one who went wrong?

Eleanor of Aquitaine Reflects on the Wildfire at Big Sur

Nearly a thousand years have passed
Since my cruel husband
And our wolfish sons
Burned the lovely Loire Valley
In their infernal lust
For land and castles and crowns.
What would I have done
If the tower where the proud Plantagenet
Kept me prisoner had caught fire?
Nineteen years in captivity
Seem like an easy dream
Compared to the horrors
Of those distant waves of flame.
And now a new conflagration far away
Threatens the earth's oldest living beings,
Toppling giant and ancient trees
Higher than the battlements of Poitiers.
At least in my imprisonment,
I was allowed to hold my harp,
To lift my voice at vespers,
To pray,
And to spend hours, indeed years,
Safe in my solitude.

Will the fire storm in that strange and mysterious land
Near a gentle, misty sea, devour the fragrant forest,
Or will it be resurrected at last, like the Loire, from the ashes,
Filled again with silent, tall and peaceful pines,
Regal crested quail and
Larks singing like troubadours?
At least the dark angels of wildfire
Are kinder than the serpents of war.
I would have welcomed the flames to my tower
In exchange for the eternal carnage
My husband and sons have wrought.

Dorothy Wordsworth Vents in Blank Verse*

Why, yes, of course I saw them first, but I
See everything before he does, not just
The yellow jonquils swaying in chorus
Across lake Windermere. I see all sorts
Of things that he does not observe—the tufts
Of lamb's wool stuck to the fence post—or clouds
So soft and sweet one almost smells the air
They drift across in the rosy morning—
A peasant girl in satin shoes tossed out
Like turnip peels by some matron who rules
A manor house. The world is so alive
With sights that take one's breath away and tear
One's heart to tatters with both joy and pain.

He is more tranquil than I am, and he
Prefers to contemplate rather than rush
Heart first into each moment's ecstasies.
My notebook is for him—to nudge his thoughts.
"Oh, William," I'll remark, "The redbreast sings
So sweetly in the sycamore." "Do make
A note of that, dear Sister," he replies.
I am so dear to him he never calls
My name without the preface, "dear." It is
My title truly, since Mrs. will not
Be mine. William could never manage a
Household without my help. Dove Cottage is
Our home, and it is I who stoke the fire
And set the breakfast kettle on the hob.
I hear the gray darlings cooing high in
The eaves, and rise in damp and cold to make

The morning golden for dear William and
His precious poetry. I pack the pork
And mustard in the basket for noontime
Rambles past chirping riverbanks to meet
Beloved Samuel, to greet and talk away
The afternoon amid the soaring larks
And lilacs scenting the twilight as soft
Shadows fall like a bridal veil over
The sacred faces of the primroses
Before the gray again enfolds the hushed
And wordless world in its embrace. I am
The one who follows his most certain steps
To our stone home and lights the fire again
And brings the fragrant tea, glistening like stones—
Like the river pebbles in his cup. "Your scones
Are peerless, dear Sister," he says to me
When settled with is pipe and his well-worn
Volume of Milton on his knee. "And no
Housewife in Grasmere could rival your tarts."

Why then, does he contrive to marry her?
He thinks he pleases me by choosing one
Who was my childhood friend. Mary is sweet
Indeed, but how can I convey to him
How plain and uneventful is her mind?
And with dear Caroline, his love-child back
In France, the issue of his foolish youth,
What need has he of more children? They will
But intercept the spark that flickers in
His mind when I notice the sound of cows

Lowing softly through the rolling fog, or small
Rabbits hiding among the ruined steps
Of the old priory? If children were
About, there would be squeals to drown the dear
Shy doves, and mean little boots stomping on
The helpless moss. Where will tranquility
Be then? And when the time for penning lines
In recollection with our quiet thoughts
That hover in the dusk like whispers of
Our mother, dead these decades now, but still
Humming amid our sibling dreams?

And yet, my happiness is nothing next
To his. My notebooks and the daily flow
Of scones and cakes and tea, like water in
The River Wye, are all for him. Within
My rocky bed I babble on, that he
May hark the bard, proclaim a choir among
The dancing daffodils.

Author's note: Dorothy Wordsworth, sister of the British Romantic poet, William Wordsworth, lived her entire life with her brother, even after he married and had five children. She cared for his children and his household and made her notebooks, filled with observations of nature and human activities, available to her brother. He relied upon them heavily in composing his poems, including his famous, "I Wandered Lonely as a Cloud." In middle age, Dorothy became completely insane and at times violent. She lived into her eighties and was cared for by her brother until his own death five years before hers.

Black and White

Outside, spring's white moon
Broods over the jasmine
And over the streaked skunks,
Darting from darkness
Like shadow puppets,
Black and white in their shy splendor.

Inside, the white cats sleep on their backs,
Their paws bent over their round bellies.
One of them makes little noises
Like the soft breeze stroking the skunks
And touching winter's last white camellias.

A blossom drops in the darkness,
The stars seem like so many petals,
And the cats and the moon
Breathe the same hushed breath.

Elizabeth Barrett Browning in Florence

On my first day in Florence, I saw more penises
(Or is it properly Peni?)
Than I had seen in all my life before,
Though admittedly, I had seen none,
Invalid that I was, shut-in for all those infernal years
Till Robert's flame phoenixed me
Into the sun-blessed goddess I've become.
So to be more exact, I have seen one male appendage,
His of course, though dimly, under the covers.
England's passions pale here in the land of naked statues—
Male bodies pulsing with sinews, muscles,
And huge, shoeless feet.
The British wear boots.

What was I to do, staggered as I was
By marble torso after marble torso, shoulders, biceps,
Trouserless legs? Even the churches are filled
With muscle-bound saints.
At first I thought the Florentines had unlocked
The secret dreams of women—
> A beating heart in a hard chest
> Pressed against her face,
> Strong fingers clutching the small of her back—
> Hot breath like the west wind on the nape of her neck
> And a presence, so tall and solid holding her,
> Whispering his deep need,
> How only she can lead him to the heights—
> And he would die
> Would spill every drop of his blood
> To protect her from warriors with swords.

That is what I thought
In those first heady days in Florence
When Robert and I held hands
Even in the Cathedral and
Saw every statue, every painting,
And every great man's grave.
Until one Sunday in the Palazzo, the bells from the Duomo
Peeling over the rooftops, as together we gazed
First at Neptune, huge and naked in his fountain,
And then at Perseus, his young, perfect body
Gleaming in the sun—
It was then that I noticed next
The head of Medusa, less beautiful than his own,
Hanging from his perfect hand,
And nearby, two heavily muscled male bodies,
Ravishing a Sabine woman—
Her head held back,
Unimportant.

My eyes opened then, as
The yellow Tuscan noon light
Bathed every inch of marble in this city,
Art's citadel.
It was then that I saw each statue
Lovingly chiseled by the hands of men.
I saw Michael Angelo in his workshop,
Looking long and longer
At a perfect naked boy,
Stroking the stone, conceiving how to make
The firm flesh even more exquisite in rock.

I saw this Florence, the barracks of Dante, of Galileo,
Donatello, Cellini, Machiavelli—
This place of music and color and craft—
This universe of men, and men and men
Revolving in planetary orbits
Around other men—
And not a single woman
Even a distant moon.

Queen Liliuokalani's Farewell

I offer you, my people, this song of farewell;
I heard the melody in my sorrowing heart.
I pray that all the *ohanas* in these holy islands
Will sing it always—
That the *keiki* will learn it from the *kupuna*
For years to come.
I have no other gift for you, as
Tomorrow I will no longer be your Queen.
They have called me a criminal and
Sentenced me to hard labor,
Though I am a mother, and my only crime
Is loving you.
How these businessmen hate motherhood!
They steal the mother whales
From our generous seas
And kill them in sight of their babies
Who will die in the deep waters
Without their mothers to feed and guide them.
They bring hungry dogs in their ships
And let them loose on our soft beaches
To attack the baby monk seals
Nursing in peace with their quiet mothers.
My old friend, Queen Victoria of Britian,
Can do nothing to halt these usurpers,
As she is old now, and frail, but blessed
Because her subjects have not betrayed her.
America has unseated all their native Kings,
Chief Joseph of the Nez Perce and all the others,

And now they thirst for more land beyond the seas
And more nations to eradicate.

Though these Americans live among us, they hate
All that we are: our hulas, our chants and
Our talk stories, even our food
And our beautiful brown bodies.
What would their grandfathers think,
The ones who came with their black hats
With their Bibles in their thin, bony hands?
They brought their Jesus, and we welcomed him,
As hospitality has always been the Hawaiian way.
The Buddha's children also came to live with us;
They are part of our *ohana* now. They brought
Their own dances and their own chants.
Every summer they gather to honor their ancestors
In the ancient way, as the missionaries from America
And their descendants never did.
I have read the Bible they brought, and I see
These descendants as the new Pharisees,
Living only for self-aggrandizement and gain.
Thieves and criminals themselves, they have set out
To crucify me. But I must not harden my heart.
Like Jesus, I must remain silent.
I have no weapons, and as your mother
I have no wish for war, as I cannot bear the thought
Of injury to any of you.

I must trust that President McKinley will redress
This wrong, that American Justice will prevail,
Though I am a prisoner now in an empty room
In the lovely Iolani Palace, with no books,
No newspapers, nothing but a pencil to write down
This song. This song is for you.
Carry it, my children, in your breath.
I will never forget you, as you are as sweet to me
As the scent of wild plumeria, as precious as the *honu*—
The sea turtle whose babies are born
On our sacred shores.
Mahalo for honoring me as your monarch,
Though I am crowned with thorns.
Let us sing our song together.
Let it be my last Aloha as your Queen.

A Sonnetish Valentine

For my niece, Kathleen

For some, the day of Valentine brings tears
And fears, and thoughts of loss and long regret,
Of nights alone with no one near for kind
And thoughtful words and whispering, the scent
Of crimson roses shared in the soft air,
The sound of Mozart's golden notes to hear
And talk about, and none to sense the heart
Beating in tandem with the hearts of all
The cupids and the doves and friends of good
Intent. It is the heart that binds us up
And lifts us past the sense of loneliness.
In chocolates, cookies, wild red valentines,
We celebrate the dented circle with
No end, the scarlet ribbon running through us all.

Dream Girl

A portrait of Mufide Kadri (1819–1912)

In the fading days of Ottoman glory,
A magic child was born.
Her life was the stuff that dreams are made of
And ancient mythic legends portray.
An orphaned baby taken in by the barren wife of
An elegant and patrician man, this precious girl
Grew up in old Constantinople, sheltered
By date palms and whitewashed walls.
Her doting adoptive father provided her
With tutors and teachers
Of the highest caliber—violin virtuosi and pianists.
By the age of ten, she learned to paint professionally
Like Renoir and Monet, beautiful, dreamy light-filled
Visions of happy, respected women and men,
Reading, playing music, strolling in the sunlight
In the finest European clothing.
She won prizes, held her head high as the first
Woman art teacher in Turkey. But in all this worldly glory,
Still pure and holy, what went on in her secret heart?

Her final painting, *Lovers on the Beach,*
Depicts a man and a woman in creamy white clothing,
The lady wearing a French style chapeau.
Walking near the shallows, the handsome man holds her arm as
They stroll together and looks at nothing but her.
All is gauzy and golden, the sun sparkling
Across the rosy waves as they gently lap the sand,
Almost touching the hem of the lady's ruffled frock.

In the distance, the clock tower chimes its soft sound,
Speaking only with the waves,
Saying nothing about time.
In this vision, his love will linger forever,
And he will be handsome always,
Cherishing her unceasingly.
Alas, like Keats, England's Golden Boy before her,
Sweet Mufide died young, unmarried, childless, and Turkey
Fell to ruins. But everything she left behind
Was beautiful.

The Gambler's Lover in the Rat Pack Days

It's Halloween, shortly after five, and the evening feeling
Has already started to settle in. Here in Las Vegas,
From the balcony of our room at the Stardust, my gaze darts
Down at an odd rooftop—heat vents, air conditioning units,
Mottled asphalt, a carelessly thrown away broom—
Who could have left it there? From the floor below mine,
The smell of cigar smoke wafts upward.
I remember the hotel in Monte Carlo. The balcony there
Came out over the sea, the waves lapped all night,
And the evenings were long and warm.
We ate croissants in the morning air,
And he won at every game he played.
He is even here. But the cab driver who brought us back
From Caesar's was giving his riders Mars Bars
For trick or treat, just as I was craving
Something sweet.

The sky has darkened a little now. There's a crescent moon,
And Venus is out beyond. Slender palm trees silhouette
Just above the horizon, and a strange gold glow
Covers the foothills. The signs at the Silver Slipper
And the Frontier flash on and on, and even the Greyhound
Bus sign looks like a casino, with its blue, neon outlined dog
Revolving forever. A real dog barks somewhere in the desert.
Some early partiers are already out on the street.
One woman is dressed as a spider with eight arms.
If I could choose a costume, I would be the Magician
And wand myself away from this place.

Gracie in the Sixties

A prose poem

Gracie had a grand piano in her family room. Her father was a doctor, and they lived in a custom-built house, out among the orchards past Penitencia Creek. The kids in our school lived in tract houses, on farms or orchards. Now, if you should drive by Gracie's house, the place looks weathered, and of course the pear trees have evolved into subdivisions of two-storied houses, more expensive than Gracie's ever was.

When Gracie was a sophomore, she ran with me and the other seniors. She got to ride shotgun in Bill Kelly's souped-up dragster, wearing his Letter Sweater with all his medals, chugging a Coke and turning back the glances of the boys from Bellarmine, out for the evening in their dad's XKE. Gracie took Bill away from the head cheerleader at James Lick High, who had loved him since they were kids together in kindergarten. Gracie dropped him a week later, and the cheerleader wouldn't take him back. When we were all away at college, I heard Gracie ran off with the history teacher and was mentioned in his divorce.

Gracie's mother looked vaguely like a cameo and owned a string of real pearls. Her father never spoke to any of us, even at the party that Gracie had our last autumn together. It was her mother who bustled about, fussing with the pizza and the planning. I came early, to help too, in the afternoon. Gracie's mother had just washed her silver hair and rolled it up. I'll never forget that dazzling arrangement, each geometric section, tidily divided, neatly coiled over those wire mesh rollers, held in place by metal clippies. And her bangs were curved over a length of cotton then taped to her forehead, immaculately.

I remember how exquisite her coiffure would look when she combed it out. But that night, when Gracie's mother poked her head into the family room to make sure everyone was behaving, her hair looked so ordinary, just brushed back with a few undistinguished wisps of bangs.

At that moment, we were fooling around at the piano, the one Gracie had practiced on since she was three; we knew she had held recitals, played pieces by Beethoven for invited guests, her parents' friends, not us. But when we asked her to play "Love Me Tender" that autumn evening, she couldn't get through it without eight or nine mistakes.

I only saw Gracie once after she graduated. She had pierced her ears and flunked out of Berkeley. Her hair had grown well below her waist and was wild and wavy. She had her arms around two young men who looked like the Beatles, and she hardly seemed to remember my name. I suppose she broke the history teacher's heart.

Greta in the Eighties

She buys children's books
For herself and writes, "For Greta" inside.
With her old Nikon, she snaps exquisite shots
Of the roses she has planted in her garden
Through all her years as a grownup;
She captures the dewdrops on the petals,
All the shades from mauve to twilight gold.
She listens to Abba's "I have a Dream"
Over and over in her Volkswagen
Until her divorce,
Her fourteen-year-old son
Who won't go to school,
And the married man she loves
Blur into a roseate fog,
And she floats in a warm sea in the moonlight,
Wearing a long gauzy gown
With lace at the wrists
And a heart-shaped locket at her throat.

When the music fades, she finds herself
On the freeway, a huge truck beside her,
"Jack Parkins, Sedalia, MO" painted on the door.
Jack's hand dangles from his high window;
He flips an ash toward her Rabbit
With his hairy fingers.
Greta's jaw tightens.
She remembers the farm back in Germany
When her father killed the pig
Without telling her.

Seeing Him

A man and a woman drive toward Mendocino;
His hands grip the wheel of his silver Porsche,
His eyes fixed on the chill blue coast.
She remembers their tennis date the week before—
The way he beat her, then deftly
Jumped the net and smirked down at her face,
How he bent and kissed her as his fingers
Closed slowly around the back of her neck.
He lights a cigarette, and the smoke curls toward her.
She notices the tendons around his knuckles,
The long line of sinews up his arm
And wishes she were back in her apartment,
Washing her hair.
She thinks of the look in his eyes
The day she first saw him.
The golden eyes of an old wild animal
Would have been warmer;
A seat on a silver space craft
Surging out toward Uranus
Would have put her more at ease.

Betrayal

        Five Years Old:

She stands beside the big loud wringer
Washing machine,
So much taller than she.
The sound it makes, over and over again,
Sloshing the clothes back and forth,
On and on, carries a sadness
That crashes down on her like a hot cyclone.
She has to tell someone.
"I feel like I don't have any mommy or daddy," she says.
Her mother, on the other side of the washer,
Looks down at her.
"Who do you think I am, the washer woman?"
The girl has no answer.
Soon she will learn
To stay silent.

Eight Years Old:

She has become a child who sleeps late
With her head under the ratty old quilts.
No one ever comes to wake her,
Though there are people in the house.
Finally, she wanders into the kitchen
And eyes the cereal boxes, haphazard on the counter,
And the neat line of ants focused on a glob of glistening jam.

Outside, her hair uncombed,
She sees a sweet toddler,
Rosy and round in clean new clothes.
She wants to slap him and make him cry,
But instead, she turns to the hillside
Behind the buildings, sits in the dirt
And watches grasshoppers.
She has spoken to no one,
Though her mind is filled with thoughts.
Alone with the insects, at least
The thing that makes bad dreams is not near her now.

Sixty Years Old:

How glorious the red maples are in spring, she thinks,
How stunning the deep pink azaleas.
She walks under the new oak leaves,
Sees the robins bouncing on bushes
Just before twilight.
"How lovely it all is," she mumbles in her mind,
Until the dove, invisible in the shadowy branches,
Calls over and over in sad, slow tones,
The sound she heard so long ago
When the wound came
And everything grew dark.

Barbie and Ken's Divorce

Five-year-old Zaya brings Barbie to Grandma's house
For their Saturday play date. Barbie wears her white lace
Wedding gown. Zaya announces, "Barbie got divorced.
She was married to Ken, but today she married Jack.
You can get divorced and marry someone else
And have another wedding whenever you want."
Grandma takes a slow breath and turns away.
She reflects on the sixty years of her marriage
To Zaya's grandpa, puttering now in the garden.
She remembers their struggles,
Moments when they might have given up,
But their long love lasted.
She wipes her tears with her apron, so Zaya won't notice.
Then Grandma gazes out to the bird house
Where the same wrens return every year.
Her parents must have told her they're both
Divorced and re-married like her other grandparents,
She muses. She turns to her granddaughter
And starts to speak, but stops as she realizes,
Zaya wouldn't even be here if they had kept their promises.

Joan on the Mower

She was born in the Gold Country
Long after the gold was gone.
After Stanford, she traveled to Mexico
And Spain, the home of California's Conquistadores,
And learned what Fascism can do, even today.
She became an expert on the Ohlone, the Missions
And Junipero Serra, all the good and bad
Of the Golden State's long existence—its glorious
Rocky coasts, its redwoods, sequoias and pines,
Its sun-burnished poppies in spring, snowy Sierra,
And the hot Mojave. She has seen the swallows
And the Monarchs, the golden-eyed cougars,
The bears at Yosemite, the horned toads, the sea lions
And the adorable sea otters, snacking on their backs
In the waves.

In spring, she will turn ninety, and she has observed it all.
Last year for her birthday, she bought herself a Ford X150
To haul all the weeds to the green waste dump.
This year she has a riding mower to manage the grasses on
Her homestead on the road to Tahoe. Her big black dog sits
Beside her, and as they mow, they have time to think and
View the snow on the foothills of the Sierra along with
The smog and heat waves over in Sacramento.

"I decided I want to die on my John Deere mower,"
Her latest text tells me. Another storm is coming
From the north, a new atmospheric river, and the
Fish in her pond don't know what season it is.
She's not depressed. The poppies will show up
Eventually, and the sweet brown quail are always around.

Deep Blue

Four months without rain
And every plant but the sturdy cypress
Wilts in the September dusk.
Even at nine, the air is still and heavy.
The dog lets his tongue dangle;
The hot horizon glows the color of old parchment.
She stands in the yard under a brittle elm;
A tired camellia droops in the shadows.
This morning, she went to a funeral
At the big hot church around the corner.
The daughter of an old friend died at nineteen.
The people in the pews stared blankly
As rainbow colored light floated
From the stained-glass window, and lingered
On the statue of the Virgin
As a young priest from Vietnam spoke
Slowly and quietly about grace.
The dead girl's father, lost in grief,
Left before the guests could greet him.
Didn't know who had come
To help him on his way.

A soft puff of autumn breeze lifts a lock of her hair.
She tilts her head, and the stars,
Like a sudden shower, bathe her.
The cobalt sky shows her Ravenna
And the mosaics in the tiny chapel—
Dull, dry brick outside—
Within, a new universe of dazzling light.

V.
PLACES AND PEOPLE

Tucson

It could have happened in Tucson,
When families get into their cars on August evenings
And drive to the dusty park
Where swing chains squeak and children speak
In Spanish, and grownups sing sometimes.
But mostly everyone shares that impersonal
Summer sadness. Like a knife never sharpened,
It edges the outer skin.
Dry as the concrete bottom of the public swimming pool,
Unfilled for reasons long forgotten,
It makes a father of five strong children
Suddenly want to run like a puma
Back to Oaxaca—to his mother, slim at twenty-five,
Her hair braided like a black crown, Esperanza,
Always calling him Mijo, always offering
Hope and a glimpse of glory,
Even back there in that dusty place.
Instead, he sits on a crooked picnic table,
His guitar quiet on his lap, and wonders
What kind of glory his sons have longed for
Pushing the swing sometimes
Almost over the bar.

August Back Then

For Corliss Greene

There is something about a hot night
That isn't ever going to cool off—
No gentle breeze around ten at night,
No fog rolling in.
This isn't San Francisco.
This is Mississippi,
Or someplace else a long time ago
Before engineers grabbed control
Of the air we breathe—
Before the big refrigerated Walmarts
Killed the animal in us.
This is the kind of place
Where people walk over to the minimarket
On the corner at midnight for an Eskimo Pie,
Where a man can go through a gallon of sweet tea
Before the baseball game is done,
Where the dogs live in a hell all their own,
And women put on those flimsy summer dresses
And don't even think about underwear.
Then even the polite ladies say, "Screw it!
I ain't fryin' no chicken tonight!"
There's something edgy about those steamy evenings
That makes you want to get out your old
Otis Redding records and sing along,
Makes you want to go out dancing

With a guy you know is no good
Just because he's got an air-conditioned Impala
With a cooler in the back seat full of root beer.
People take risks on nights like this—
They get sick of their own sweat
And run away from home.
They write a letter to someone
Who broke their heart way back when,
And even stick a stamp on it.
And after they've kicked off the sheets
For the tenth time just before the doves wake up,
Those mournful heralds of another hot dawn,
They start to wonder
If they could have been wrong about God.

Mt. McKinley

Some call it Mount Denali now,
As the Athabascans did.
"There is the Big One, Denali," the native people said,
Looking up from their sunken dwellings,
Lined with willow to control the cold.
The women gazed at the two-faced mountain
As they rubbed the moose hide between their knuckles
And pulled the sinews from the caribou's foreleg
For sewing thread.

There are six of us in the airplane;
The little girl next to the pilot has fallen asleep.
Her parents paid one hundred dollars
For her to see the Big One.
We fly over the tundra,
Cross sluggish, glacier-fed rivers,
Leaving the golden grizzly behind,
And there, on one of five clear days this summer,
We see it, huge and threatening,
Its two summits covered in snow
That could linger a thousand years.
Reticular clouds hover only over Denali;
"The mountain creates its own weather," says our pilot.

The Athabascans never thought of climbing it.
They tracked the snow hare
And prayed to the Great Spirit
That they might not starve in the winter.
This spring, our pilot tells us,
Two Japanese climbers
Fell into a snow drift and died,
And two Swiss mountaineers
Fell asleep for the last time
From hypothermia.
The long northern sunlight settles an aura
On the Big One, as the cameras try to capture her.
I ask the Great Spirit to forgive me
For coming here.

At the Mission

At Carmel Mission
The hydrangeas are huge
And the bougainvillea climbing the adobe
Surges with color, even in summer mist.
Inside the dark basilica, white tapers
Leave waxy droplets
On the wrought iron candelabra,
And the paintings of the Stations of the Cross
Among the murky walls are too dim to discern.
The pilgrim must simply remember
Each step along the way.
Her foot slides along the cool stony tiles,
Past the tall Spanish candle holders of intricate silver.
Nearing the altar, she kneels
Before the tabernacle, deeply recessed beyond the rail.
Her eyes rest on the almost indiscernible inscription
On the stone flooring:
"Padre Junipero Serra."
On the wall behind her and to the right,
An enormous image of the Virgin of Guadalupe
Surrounded by a nimbus of blue and gold
Radiates like a throbbing poppy,
Warming the cold adobe
And the bones at rest.

Californians

All we had ever known was sunshine.
The sky was always the gentle blue
Of faded Levi's while little wisps of white
Drifted sometimes, harmlessly.
In the south, sweet oranges and creamy avocados
Grew on those plump, casual trees.
In the north, the orchards bloomed every spring
With tart apricots and generous almonds.
Even the shopping centers had names like
The Pruneyard and El Paseo,
Places where all we amiable people could sip
White wine from the Livermore Valley,
Munch on Monterey Jack,
Or stroll through tiled sidewalks
In our tank tops,
Feeling the warmth on our bare arms,
Thriving with the poppies and the marigolds,
Liking the azaleas and the deep pink fuchsias
In the easy shade.

What were we to do when the rains came,
When the nights got dark and long,
And we had to stoke the fire,
Burn real wood for warmth,
When gray was the color every morning,
And nothing but water, cold, hard water,
Filled every crevice,
When tempests blew heavy branches

Through our windows,
And houses started slipping into the sea?

What about the others who suffered—
The redwoods whose roots are ruined, the feral cats
Haggard and hungry, the baby skunks flushed away
From their mothers? Do we listen,
Past the crashing sound of the deluge
To the urgent siren of frogs
Far in the back of the garden?

Mexico

Darling Mexico, you are always in my heart;
The joy you have given me, from my earliest memories
To the long, lovely years of my golden time
Lifts me up and carries me, like the eagle on your flag,
Through the tearful times, through sorrow and loss.
There is nothing bland in Mexico; you are red, yellow and green.
You are corn, you are avocados, you are flaming chilis.
You are loud Mariachi music, filled with exultation, even
At a funeral.
You are the Virgin of Guadalupe, wrapped in roses,
You are some of the best foods I have ever eaten, always warm,
Always alive with lime and jalapenos and oozing with glorious
Golden cheese.

Spain stole all your gold,
And the rest of the world routinely treats you like dirt,
Especially your snooty neighbors to the north.
Yet you hold your head high, walk in dignity and respect.
You know your ancient people invented mathematics,
Astronomy and the calendar.
You know it's all about envy.
The Belgians and the Swiss, frozen with jealousy
In their stony cold chalets,
And the imperious French, who claim to have invented
Mousse and ganache, try to make it all about themselves.
But you know Montezuma was not born in Belgium
And there is not a single Cocoa tree in Europe.
You know you gave chocolate to the world.
And those of us who live for your beautiful brown elixir
Will never stop loving you!

Borobudur

How long did Borobudur lay under the vines?
Each day the foliage grew wilder over the stones;
Dark glistening leaves covered the scenes
Of Holy Buddha's life, carved by patient fingertips.
Moist mosses crept through time
Up stair after stair, at last
Spreading over every image
Of the Great One's secret smile.
Blossoms dropped, and birds found food
At the temple's very top.
Finally, the jungle held every step in its twining arms
While serpents coiled around the banyan's huge shoulders
And high-flying lorikeets saw nothing but green, green, green.

It was a time for sediment, for settling of stones,
And the Buddha napped, long and deep,
Dreaming green and fragrant dreams.
Wings flitted over his third eye for centuries
And the scent of sweet gardenia
Smoldered like incense in the warm tomb.

But light once kindled bides its time,
And darkness can never master it.
Great Gautama's awakening travels a circling path,
Truer than the snake's twisting, or the vine's grip.
He pulls his pilgrims back to the forest's deepest core.

Costa Comes Home

We watched a soccer game in Patmos—
The waiters from our Greek cruise ship
Against the locals, who had somehow imported
A Brit who was better than the rest.
Costa, the charismatic cocktail waiter
Who was known to sing along with the floor show,
Even dancing among the tables at times
And making the ladies smile,
Was kicked out for pushing an opponent
In a down-right rowdy way. As a result,
Our crew had to play short-handed,
And their perfect record of wins was finally broken.
Sailing back to Athens, Costa never heard the end of it.
But he felt no shame,
And just kept smiling his historic smile.

However, Costa is not the hero here. Patmos is.
Don't be ashamed that you have never heard
Of this tiny island, closes to Rhodes,
Not too far from Turkey.
Had I heard of it before the ship docked?
You probably wouldn't sense it by viewing
The town's two tavernas and the pure dirt
Soccer field, but something uncharacteristic
Happened here a long time ago.
Now you're guessing.
No, Socrates didn't drink his hemlock here,
And the Colossus of Rhodes
Certainly was not built on Patmos.
You'll never get it, even if you went to Sunday school.

But the next time you find yourself off on business,
Lodged at the Holiday Inn, the wife and kiddies
Snug at home, reach into the dresser drawer
And pull out the Gideons Bible.
Then turn to the last mad chapter
Where John the Divine conjures up a vision
Of the Holy Queen of the Sea, clothed with the sun,
The moon beneath her feet, her head
Crowned with twelve stars
Filling the black Mediterranean sky,
And angels in combat with the most evil
Dragon of all.
Can you believe all those fiery angels,
All those foaming horses?
Where could this apocalypse have come from?
Patmos.

After two weeks of wearing white jackets
And waiting on middle-aged Californians,
Those young Greeks ran around that soccer field
With a fury I had never witnessed, never been close to.
Costa was the wildest of all.
Was it different for John?
High above the oleanders, held prisoner,
His eyes undoubtedly looked deeper than the dirt
That still composes Patmos.
At dusk he saw the sun
Like an azalea in a hot wind finally fall;
At night the horses came flaming into the sky.

Osaka Castle: Summer Solstice

Everything is a dream.
Man's ambition is but a dream of dreams.
With grand Osaka in my mind,
I must vanish like the dew.
—General Hideyoshi Toyotomi's deathbed tanka

A cloudiness, this side of the veil from rain
Mists the city in a silk scarf;
The moat around the castle
Takes on the deep luster of celadon.
With the sun in seclusion,
No light sparkles the water as it shifts
In quiet turns of shadow.
The huge and ancient walls
Are gray pearls, glowing moist,
Clothed in old mosses and vines.
The castle ascends in the center
Of a thousand skyscrapers, spread out like pebbles
In a circle of respect.
The roof and walls, all pyramids and points,
Are eight stories of glory,
Garnished in dolphins of fresh gold,
Thrusting their tails into the infinite gray of heaven.
The highest green tiles, the shade of June melon,
Echo the damp taste of summer on the tongue,
Evoke Hideyoshi and four hundred years
Gone like the dream of a dream.

A heron glides past the castle
His feet straight behind him
Like an arrow dipped in dew.

Planning a Spring Reunion

The two who organize everything are at it again.
A while back it was dim sum at the big place up the peninsula
And Elton John at the Cow Palace.
A few years later it was Original Joe's
And the Rolling Stones at the San Jose Arena
When the Sharks were out of town.
The most recent took place at the sandy dunes of Asilomar
With a Saturday golf tournament,
Three foursomes over at Del Mar.
"It's time for another reunion," they remind us,
And this time they have their eyes on Arizona—
The same twelve old pals, because compatibility is everything.
It'll be just like old times—
Tacos and sangria with Margaritas
And a few puffs on the back porch at sunset.
The usual twelve, two vans, the changing colors of the desert,
The quiet twilights, the rugged bluffs,
Rustic showers in the heat of the day,
Shadows down in the canyons,
Sleeping bags under the magic sky.
"Nothing could be more beautiful," they tell me.
"You have to come." They pass a bottle of Chenin Blanc;
Smoke rises from fingertips.
I think of Basho, gazing up at the Milky Way
As it arched over the sea to Sado Isle;

I think of Van Gogh in that swirling blue night
With stars and more stars glittering down
On the silent sunflowers.
My mind wanders to Soledad Mission
Settled in the dusty San Juaquin Valley
For two hundred years with a bell that still rings
And scruffy dry rose bushes that still bloom.
The eleven who will travel to Arizona,
My precious old pals,
How can I help them understand
That my soul has surrendered to solitude?

Ala Moana Park

It's big, but not huge like Central Park or
Golden Gate Park, or even Balboa Park in old
San Diego, housing the best zoo in the world,
Where the animals are loved and rescued
Before they become extinct. No, Ala Moana Park
Isn't that big, but it has a massive footprint and its own
Mana, its own sacred
Vocation. I left out the park's middle name:
Beach. Yes, the beach is part of the park, so maybe
Ala Moana Beach Park is even bigger than all the rest,
Since it has an ocean attached.
The surfers show up before the pink dawn and linger
Long after the catamarans catch the red sunset in their sails.
Families and children splash in the tide pools and wiggle
Their toes in the golden sand. Sea turtles stick their noses
Out of the waves, the golden plover, just arrived
From the long, cold flight from Alaska,
Plants her feet first on the sparkling sands of Ala Moana Beach,
And a monk seal leaves the sea and settles in to give birth.
On the opposite side, next to the boulevard that carries
The tourists from the airport to Waikiki and Diamond Head,
There is a murky canal where old men sit
With their fishing lines, and willows, filled with
Java sparrows and mynahs, dip their long, leafy fingers
Into the dark water as a pair of ducks floats by
And white plumeria blossoms fall all year long.

But the park's glorious crown is in its center,
The generous space where the ancient
Banyan tree forms its own mandala,
Sending out its long root tendrils like
A benevolent army of octopus, beckoning in the spirit of
Aloha—welcoming the young homeless woman who pulls
A silk scarf from her tote bag, wraps it around her shoulders
And lies down in darkness, comforted,
Safe in the Banyan's embrace.
On Sunday mornings, the drum circle
Surrounds the Banyan. Seated among the gnarly roots,
They send their sounds on old instruments out over the waves,
Into the kind sky, past the canal and up the mountain
Where the ancient chiefs are buried.
On another morning, a family boards a bus at the
Homestead Road, rides into town and stops at the park.
They cross the boulevard to Foodland, buy fresh ahi poke
And Spam musubi, a picnic lunch for the oldest boy's
Birthday. They stretch out around the Banyan,
Settle among the roots. Auntie plays her ukulele, and
Uncle, who still remembers the old chants,
Sings a blessing for the boy. The park and the Banyan
Have done their work.

Circling the World with Haiku

East from Greece to Italy

Patmos, Greece
On a hot night in / Patmos, lemons scent the air / Under the white stars.

Istanbul, Turkey
Tourists get lost in / The carpet market as the / Cruise ship sails away.

Cairo, Egypt
In the hazy dawn / Near the pyramids, neighbors / Share their breakfast beans.

Addis Ababa, Ethiopia
At the airport in / Addis Ababa, the faint / Scent of tobacco.

Zambia
A water lily / On her tusk, an elephant / Drinks in the river.

Botswana
On the Chobe, swarms / Of migrating butterflies / Float past a hippo.

Cape Town, South Africa
At the Cape of Good / Hope, brown rocks jut from the green / Sea. Seals nod their heads.

Near Jerusalem, Israel
The tour guide locks the / Bus so the tourists will shop / At the diamond store.

Dubai, United Arab Emirates
    Skyscrapers of all / Shapes form Dubai's skyline; tan / Dust everywhere else.

Mumbai, India
    All night, fireworks boom / Over Mumbai Bay in the / Bright Diwali lights.

Near Delhi, India
    A boy herds the cows / Down the center of the road / On his bicycle.

At the Bandavgarh Tiger Reserve, India
    A tiger turns her / Back on the tourists and growls / As she walks away.

Kathmandu, Nepal
    At the gold stupa, / Prayer flags flutter and monkeys / Eat each other's lice.

Bangkok, Thailand
    At the Great Buddha / Temple, a tourist is asked / To remove his hat.

Near Saigon, Vietnam
    Even as darkness / Falls, farmers in the rain plant / Their last rice seedlings.

Near Hue, Vietnam,
    Rice fields surround the / Water buffalo and the / Ancient grave markers.

Halong Bay, Vietnam
    Over Halong Bay, / Fishing hawks circle, looking / Down at the dark sea.

Near Hanoi, Vietnam
    At twilight in the / Rice field, workers bend over / Picking escargot.

The South China Sea
    The ship cruises past / Fishing buoys and a large school / Of white jellyfish.

The South China Sea, Passing the Philippines
    Out at sea, fishing / Birds swarm high in the sky, then / Dive to catch their prey.

Melbourne, Australia
    A wild cockatoo / Screams from a lamp post in the / Middle of Melbourne.

Uluru, Australia
    Tiny black frogs hop / In the huge puddles at the / Foot of Uluru.

Sydney, Australia
    At Bondi Beach an / Ibis stands on a rooftop / In the summer breeze.

Hong Kong, China
    Before dawn, the lights / Of Hong Kong and Kowloon meet / In the dark harbor.

Macau, China
    In Macau, signs in / Every shop claim to have the / Best warm egg yolk tarts.

Taipei, Taiwan
    Near the red columns / Of the War Memorial / Young guards stand with fists.

Naha, Okinawa, Japan
    In summer rain, an / Egret lands on the arched stone / Bridge over the pond.

Nagasaki, Japan
    At the Peace Park in / Nagasaki, schoolboys in / Uniform say, "Hi."

At Matsue Castle, Japan
    The castle's high gun / Turrets look down on herons' / Nests in the cedars.

Kyoto, Japan
    Clouds hover above / The Golden Temple; iris / Reflect in the pond.

Osaka, Japan
    The bride and groom at / Osaka Castle wear black / And white tennis shoes.

Tokyo, Japan
    By the Palace moat, / The first hydrangeas blossom / Near the green willows.

Busan, Korea
>The lady selling / Fish naps near the tanks of live / Eels and octopus.

Honolulu, Hawaii, USA
>A golden plover / Returns to the sea wall, the/ Long, cold flight over.

Kaaawa, Oahu, Hawaii, USA
>As the twilight sea / Turns pink, a monk seal swims north / Through the shallow tide.

Near San Diego, USA
>Under a huge oak, / Pygmy goats nibble dry grass / And golden poppies.

At the San Diego Zoo
>From his stone Kopje, / A rock hyrax, hiding, glares / At zoo visitors.

Mission San Miguel, California, USA
>Near old Mission San / Miguel, ewes and lambs graze on / The golden hillside.

Watsonville, California, USA
>In Watsonville fog, / New quinces and sweet peas scent / The cool ocean breeze.

Santa Cruz, California, USA
>California sea / Lions relax on the wharf, / Smelling the fresh fish.

Los Gatos, California, USA
   Autumn's first rain comes / In the night, washing through the / Redwoods and the oaks.

Oklahoma, USA
   Two huge hawks perch on / A fence in Oklahoma / As the trucks roll by.

Joplin, Missouri, USA
   The four o'clock train / Rolls through Joplin, whistling in / The crisp autumn air.

Key West, Florida, USA
   In the twilight, a / Pair of dolphins follows the / Cruise ship out to sea.

Cienfuegos, Cuba
   The old domed mansions / Of Cienfuegos crumble in / The winter sunlight.

Havana, Cuba
   In old Habana, / A red Impala slows down / For a horse carriage.

New York City, USA
   Under rainy gray / Skies on the gray sea, the ship / Finds the Green Lady.

Boston, USA
   A gray squirrel scampers / Over the cobblestones in / Paul Revere's courtyard.

Montreal, Canada
    Crowds of tourists fill / Notre Dame, gazing up at / The ceiling of stars.

Quebec, Canada
    The horse stamps his feet / and drinks from the fountain when / The carriage ride ends.

Halifax, Nova Scotia, Canada
    A heron feeds in / The pond near a replica / Of the Titanic.

Peggy's Cove, Nova Scotia, Canada
    Lichens grow on the / Ancient stones overlooking / The wild Atlantic.

Lisbon, Portugal
    In Lisbon, German / Tourists rush off the bus to / Buy warm egg yolk tarts.

Santiago de Compostela, Spain
    Dressed in Spanish red, / The bride's mother waits under / The grand thurible.

Madrid, Spain, at the Prado Museum
    El Greco's solemn / Knight, hand over his heart, stares / Through the centuries.

London, England
    On a summer's day / Music fills the air as the / Queen appears in green.

Preparing to Cross the English Channel
> A mouse looks for crumbs / Along the wooden floor of / St. Pancras Station.

Paris, France
> Summer rain falls through / The scaffolding on the ruins / Of old Notre Dame.

Auvers-Sur-Oise, France
> White irises fade, / But blue and yellow endure / Where Vincent once lived.

Giverny, France
> Beneath the willow, / Dragonflies hover over / The water lilies.

Rouen, France
> In Rouen, pigeons / Near the old Cathedral call / Through the cold spring rain.

Bayeux, France
> Bishop Odo wields / His mace on the Tapestry, / Slaughtering Saxons.

Pont du Hoc, France
> In the cold wind at / Pont du Hoc, a sea gull stands / Where the Rangers died.

Normandy Beach, France
> In cold, gentle rain, / The sound of "Taps" floats over / All the white crosses.

Near Prague, Czech Republic
    Czech police stop / To herd flat-horned dairy cows / Back across the road.

Vienna, Austria
    The Lipizzaner / Horses stroll from their palace / On their morning walk.

Passau, Germany
    Light rain in Passau: / By the Danube, bees flutter / In red salvia.

Budapest, Hungary
    Wild geese in cold rain / Cross the Danube above the / Chain bridge flying south.

St. Petersburg, Russia, at the Hermitage Museum
    A Russian guide speaks / Japanese as the tourists / View the da Vinci.

Moscow, Russia
    Marigolds at the / Cold Kremlin bloom beneath the / Gold domed cathedrals.

On the Volga River, Russia
    A ruined church stands / In the swollen river; birch / Trees grow through the bricks.

Milan, Italy
    Beyond the high spires / Of Milan's Duomo stand the / Distant snowy Alps.

At the Sistine Chapel
　　Pilgrims stare in awe / In the Sistine Chapel, mouths / Open, heads bent back.

The Vatican
　　Pilgrims, pigeons and / The Pope gather on a warm / Day at St. Peter's.

Rome, Italy, at the Coliseum
　　Summer light streams down / To the dark place where martyrs / Waited for lions.

Venice, Italy
　　The golden domes of / Saint Mark's and a flock of doves / Glisten in light rain.

Life on the Island

It is the most remote archipelago
On Earth, filled with rainbows and koa trees,
Yet humans have found their way
To the center of this vast sea. A thousand
Years ago, the wayfarers from ancient
Polynesia paddled through the
Dark waves, following the stars, the birds,
The currents and the tides, taro roots in
The hulls of their canoes, spears for fishing.
They built fishponds and *heiau,* sacred
Temples fashioned from lava stone where
The gods, Kane and Lono lived.
Then others came. Captain Cook was
Killed on the shore for kidnapping a chief,
But the Chinese, the Portuguese, the Filipinos
And the Japanese learned to live in the old
Way among the fragrant plumerias, the egrets
And the whales who arrived in the warm winter.
Now these islands are home to the only
Royal Palace in America, with electricity and
Indoor plumbing older than the White House, and
A symphony with a Chinese Australian Conductor
And a Korean Concert Master from France.
Portuguese doughnuts, still called *malasadas,*
Are everywhere, warm from the food trucks.

The Japanese still hold their Obon festival every
Summer at the Buddhist Temples to remember
Their ancestors. Chinatown bustles and thrives,
And the Lion Dancers stomp through the streets
With drummers, fireworks and smoke each New Year
While Filipino nurses care for the sick in every hospital.
The Natives at last are reclaiming their language,
Their chants, and their ancient dance.
Aloha still lives here, far away
From the place where anger is everywhere,
And even neighbors and friends
Are bullied and shamed.

VI.
BACK AT THE BEGINNING

Siblings

We walk in her tiny garden
And cut figs from the tree.
Her quince still looks dead and stick-like,
But she says it will bloom soon;
The red blossoms will come out
Even in winter's chill.
We three old siblings reach up high
To pick last year's sweet oranges
And peel them in the yard,
Juice dripping on our fingers
As our heads form a tight triangle
In the pale sunlight.
We three are at ease as we were
More than six decades ago
And as we are now with no one else.
And none of us mentions
That tomorrow she will not remember
That her brother and sister were here.

The War Kids

There are not as many of us as there once were—
They called us Baby Boomers because our fathers,
When they were called off to war, left their sperm behind,
Like male octopus in the deep-sea waters,
Hoping to leave a spark of life before their own expired.

We have our own set of memories shared among us,
The children of war. We remember Oleo, that strange white goo
In a plastic pillow, bigger than a kids' two hands,
With a tiny button of yellow dye in the middle.
Grandma would give it to us to get us out of her hair
While she was cooking, and we would take turns squeezing until
All the goo turned yellow, and we could pretend
It was butter, which nobody had anymore.
Oleo on Grandma's breakfast biscuits,
Bright yellow Oleo margarine on Mommy's mashed potatoes
For lunch, red Jell-O for dessert
And green Kool-Aid in the hot afternoons.

When some of our daddies finally came back,
They brought their army blankets with them,
Brown, scratchy heavy things, not soft and colorful like Grandma's
Quilts, but they were great for hanging over the clotheslines
To make a tent. And some of the daddies
Kept wearing their Army uniforms all the time.
Maybe they didn't have any clothes of their own.

Then somehow, we weren't at Grandma's anymore
But at a big rickety place that looked like an old
Army barracks with no sidewalks, just boards
Nailed together to cover the mud.

Student Housing, it was called. There were other kids there
Whose dads screamed in the middle of the night,
And the grownups would just say, "He has battle rattles."
All the dads in this new place had a new job
Called the G.I. Bill. The ones who worked in the mines or
The smelter before the war got to go to school like us,
Only their school was called a college.
Our cramped little apartments filled up with books, and our
Daddies stayed up late, smoking and reading and typing.
Tap, tap, tap on the typewriter all night long.

We were the lucky ones whose fathers came home,
And the war never got to our doorstep.
But now more bullies have emerged,
In the long line of lonely little men who love spilling blood,
And a new generation of children of war
Will have their own shared memories,
So much worse than ours.

Patriotism

I remember now. Me with a bottle of red Nehi—
Cold, condensed sweat dripping down the glass.
Fourth of July and we just got back from Joplin.
Gramp let me sit on his lap and steer.
Johnny talked him into getting us five Roman candles each,
And six cone shaped fountains,
The kind that spew gold stars deep
Into the sultry night air. Sparklers too.
After sundown, we'd hold one
In each hand, and whirl around,
Spelling our names on the black air,
Leaving red dazzle trails on our optic nerves.
And then, just before mine went out,
I'd light a new one off Johnny's and start again.
The crickets and katydids would be loud, and so would we,
Popping off firecrackers a string at a time,
Blowing up tin cans in the alley.
Yeah, I remember that little Ozark fireworks fool.

On those heady hot nights of pure joy,
Could Little Me ever have imagined
That fireworks would get outlawed
As too dangerous for children,
But a grownup could carry a machine gun into a school
And kill every kid in sight?

Thank You, Peter

Thanks to you, Peter, I got to be an
Aunt when I was still a teenager,
And I was thrilled to have a baby
To play with. You looked like a cherub
With your sea-blue eyes and moon-golden
Hair, and I was happy to carry you around,
Hugging you and smelling your sweet baby
Scent as your tears soaked my shoulders.
You cried and kept on crying, to all the
Family's surprise. Maybe you felt like a
Stranger among them, a clan
That was all about books.
Or perhaps you were born to be a seeker
And knew from the outset
That you would find your own path.
Your kindly father's luck pointed you west
When he found a job as a teacher in a town
By the sea where your mother was content
To spend her days in the library.
Your tears stopped flowing when you
Toddled over to the beach, and your eyes widened
When you witnessed the high, rolling waves,
The fishing boats bobbing in the current and
The tides rushing in and out over the golden sands
Every red dawn and violet twilight.
You had found your castle, your forever home.

Every wound that enters a man's life found healing
In the gulls' calls, the pelicans' sweeping dives
Into the crashing breakers, and you emerged a man
With no evil in you, kind like the foam that rolls gently
Over the sand crabs. Your wife and your daughters know
You love them, as you are always nearby, like the tides,
But at times you are a mystery to them, like the moon's
Secret power over the sea.

A Valentine Tanka

For My Niece, Kathleen

Egrets fly back to
Their nests as February's
Full moon gleams over
The reef. If only we could
Share this sacred white silence.

A Beginner's Guide to Baking Cakes

First of all, remember this: baking a cake is not about you.
A cake is a gift that could fall flat and fail, so stay focused.
Some experts will tell you that baking is nothing more than
Science, like a lab experiment in your chemistry class.
Certain elements are combined in a prescribed order,
Sugar, butter, eggs, flour, salt, leavening agents, and additives
Such as nuts, fruits, spices and flavorings,
If called for in the strategic plan.
Then the components are heated to the exact specifications
To achieve the desired outcome.
Others say that cake baking is a craft, based on years of practice,
Like weaving a set of place mats or throwing a pot on your wheel.
The crafter must seek out the finest materials, focus on color,
Season, aroma, texture,
Design and scale, obtain the best tools and care for them faithfully
Until the long hours of devoted research bring the project to light,
In this case perhaps a black forest cake with cherry filling and
Whipped cream, served
In the spring when deep sweet Bings are red and ripe.
Others know in their hearts that baking is an art,
Inspired by the angels themselves, as the artist in winter's
Cold fashions the Bouche de Noel on Christmas Eve with candied
Chestnuts nestled in gingered icing with white
Sugar crystals, like snow in starlight.

The experts are all wrong. And they're all right.
Baking a cake is all of these, and you are the gift giver,
Creating with your own hands and your whole open heart
Something beautiful, delicious, memorable yet ephemeral
From nothing more than the stores in your pantry.

And you, the chemist, the weaver, the painter, the architect,
Must step aside and surrender the moment your masterpiece passes
From your hands to the birthday boy,
The graduate, the bride and groom, the loved one.
But you can treasure the memory, as I remember the carrot cake
With cream cheese icing I made for my sister's birthday when
She turned seventy,
Nine years before she died. She was complicated,
And I had to make a complicated cake for her.
When you give a gift, you must think only of the recipient.
Carrots grated by hand, crushed pineapple, coconut and almonds
That had to be toasted in advance, and after the icing, when I had
Part of a large carrot left, the baking angels whispered to me,
"Decorate the top with candied carrot curls.
You can do it. We'll show you how."
These are the memories a cake baker carries in her heart.
But as a beginner, buy the *Fanny Farmer Cookbook,* pay attention
To details, like pre-heating the oven, practice your craft,
And trust the angels of art.

August Birthdays

A green acorn, with two leaves attached,
Still wearing its little crown
Plummets to earth
In the midst of hot, dusty August.
Even when summer seems eternal,
Harbingers come
Loud like this acorn,
Or soundless as the first blossom
To fade on the oleander.

We have seen sixty-four Augusts,
And how many are left to us?
There were summers when we seemed the King and Queen
And other summers when sorrow parched the long dry days.

Time will take our diadems away,
And even pain will fade
As winter's mists descend.
Partner, true love,
Stand closer beside me now
As we face together
What is to come.

Kin

For my brother, John

Autumn, a kinsman,
One who shares old stories from childhood,
Just back from a long journey alone,
Stands at the door in the morning,
Smelling of spices and hot tea.
We gather him in our arms,
Feel the energy in him
As our fingers grasp his shoulders.
We look into his earthy eyes,
Smile straight at him,
Glance over his old clean clothes,
Gold and russet plaids
He wore last year and the year before.
"Where have you been, you old rascal?"
Our voice overflows with laughter
And the old dialect of home.

A Tanka Trio

In Memory of my sister, Margaret

October arrives
And the full moon rises from
The sea while the sky
Still shimmers. Before the pink
Twilight, I hear your voice.

Mist rolls down the green
Mountain, floats through the palms and
Turns to rain over
The sea; when we were girls, my
Sister, how we loved the rain!

The dog trembles as
Lightning strikes near the house, rain
Pours and thunder cracks.
Long ago, when the storms came,
With you, I was not afraid.

Winter Dawn

For David

Darkness remains over the cold planet
Long past the time when the birds
Like to call out from their pine homes.
Even at seven, it is still a shadow world,
And the chill turns this murky dream-place
Into a strange collage
Of onyx-toned stones
And shingles, frosted the icy shade
Of breakers on a midnight sea.
Even the animals keep to their shelter,
And for me, standing alone
Under an oak that seems to breathe
Winter's own breath,
Cold fills me
Deeper than distant stars.

I think of the son who came from me
On that December night
Longer ago than some lifetimes.
Now on his birthday, he sleeps in a distant place,
A man with a man's dreams,
But always my child.

Turning Pages

Books are like breath.
They nurture, heal, fill us with wonder,
And help us grow. I cannot live without them.
Books have pages and a secret scent.
They have weight and texture.
You can turn through the pages and peek ahead.
You can make notes in the margins
Or even pull out your pink highlighter
And mark the parts that you never want to forget.
Books are life-long friends.
The only panic attack of my lifetime occurred
When I couldn't find the *Norton Anthology of English Literature* in its usual place in the center of the shelf,
The place of honor where I can reach for it
Whenever I need a dose of Keats.
Books never die. My father died,
But his *Complete Works of Geoffrey Chaucer,*
Cambridge Edition, Copyright 1933, edited by F.N. Robinson,
Will never leave me. My father's name, written in black ink
With a fountain pen, is on the first page, along with a notation
In pencil, in some clerk's handwriting: $3.60, the price
Of my dad's textbook when he took Chaucer at
The University of Kansas in 1936.
That was a lot of money during the Great Depression,
But the treasure trove of gold that book opened
Is life itself to me.

Orchids

In the old native garden
Brown lizards dart up
The mossy wall,
A green gecko languishes under the wide taro leaves,
And again, just before Easter,
Huge white orchids emerge,
Their purple throats dotted with gold,
Open to the twilight sky.
There is no fragrance,
No sound when the flowering petals lift in the trade winds,
But there is a beauty that carries me away through the decades.

I remember the lilacs in Idaho, heavy clusters
Of purple and white in the cold spring air,
Bending down toward my little hands from the tall black bushes,
Sending a scent so heady and sweet, more joyful than
The happiest hope.

Times and places later, when my wedding day came,
I wanted lilacs for my bouquet, wanted their fragrance
To embrace me as I stepped onto a new and unknown path.
But the lilacs were gone by June, faded like the cherry blossoms,
And I remember nothing now of the random flowers
I held in my barely grown-up hands as I promised my life away.

Now old and still with the boy who gave me everything but lilacs,
We gaze at the pure white orchids glowing in the violet twilight
In the crotch of a grizzled old tree
As the Lenten moon rises over the ancient volcano.
Tears surprise me, and I almost sense the fragrance
Of lilacs long ago.

An Irish American Meets Herself

We studied Yeats and his spirals then
Only for the hollow high
Of a blue book victory.
Then, the old, wattled wizard
Meant as much to us as the allegory
In the *Faerie Queene,*
And Ireland has always been
A long way away.
But how about now—
After spinning from spring to spring
And falling into another autumn
Only to find ourselves
Dizzy at the discovery
Of us
Back at the beginning?

Shifting

You were my boyfriend when we were fifteen
When the white blossoms from the orchards covered the
Valley every spring, and all summer long the smell of hot tomato
Paste floated over Highway 101 all the way to Gilroy,
And the garlic scent rolled back.
The girls in our high school cut cots in the drying sheds
As soon as school was out, and the boys,
You and my brother, worked at the Contadina Cannery.
I thought we were the coolest couple on campus,
Cruising up Alum Rock to Santa Clara Street every night
To Mel's Drive in your candy apple Bonneville for a cherry
Orangeade. Our counselors didn't think so. The Boys' Counselor
And the Girls' Counselor took us aside,
Separately, and told us that Japanese boys weren't supposed
To date white girls. They were left over from the Second World
War, so we ignored them of course, not even noticing that we
Were among the first.

Then things started to happen.
The Tsukuda boys, who had to tape up their tennis shoes to stay on
The basketball team, told us that their parents sold the farm and
Became millionaires. The orchards disappeared too, and computers
Appeared out of nowhere.
You and the other smart boys who wore slide rules on their belts
Were ready. You bought an HP calculator with your savings from
Pumping gas and washing windows.
I was ready too, after a lot of studying, and I morphed
From a carefree Prom Queen to a professor, a speaker, a listener.
When the new college was built in the foothills

Where a pear orchard used to be, I taught thousands
Of Vietnamese refugees who showed up after another war,
Traumatized, heartbroken, lost.
We all had to become somebody else.

And now, sixty years later, we are leaping once more
To a warm place where the frost that made the apricots bloom will
No longer hinder our aching bones.
Now, you are more than a handsome boy in a white tuxedo at the
Senior Ball, more than just another Silicon Valley Entrepreneur.
Now you are the man who watches with me as the tiny crescent
Moon rises over Venus while the high tide and the trade winds
Rush in to take the beach away.
Now we live among the egrets, the first to arrive with the ripe
Tomato dawn over the sea, the last to return to
Their nests in the mangroves
When the candy apple twilight animates the waves.
You have given me a puppy to grow old with us
In the fragrant days of the white plumeria
Until the next shift arrives, and we must become
Someone else again.

Time

You just know you could never
Really run out of paper clips.
Not completely.
There always have to be two or three
Stuffed in the back of the junk drawer
Under the worn-out emery boards
And dried-up black felt marking pens.
Or even on the stepped-on loops
Of the rarely vacuumed shag carpet,
There will inevitably be a few.
You begin your search with confidence,
Finding thumbtacks, pennies, eraserless pencils,
Flattened matchbooks, the extra house key
You thought was lost.
Your fingers move faster through the upholstered buttons
That fell off the dining room chairs,
Red rubber bands, smudged from newspapers,
Antique green stamps.
A thought interrupts,
And you sit down temporarily
To add a few items to this week's grocery list
And free yourself from facing the fact
That there is not a single paper clip left.

Elegy for Auntie: *A Triversen*

On her one-hundredth
Birthday, our last Auntie eats
Five shortbread cookies.

In the wet winter,
At one-hundred and one, she
Takes her final breath.

Hawks soar in the green
Spring as the family gathers
Among the poppies.

Her youngest niece reads
About Auntie's time in the
Concentration camp.

The elders in black
Bow to her photo, among
The purple orchids.

The family feasts on
Rice and teriyaki like
Auntie always did.

Remembering Rwanda

An Anniversary Poem

It was a long time ago, before neighbors hacked each other
To pieces with machetes, red blood flooded the farmlands,
And almost a million people died. We just wanted
To meet the gorillas,
To enter their quiet world and sit with them in silence.
Seven people a day were allowed into
The mountain rain forest where these huge
Peaceful creatures lived. We rode for hours
On a flatbed truck with ten men from the village,
Our escorts—one man for each visitor to protect us
From scratches and falls, snakes and stings
When we arrived in the pathless jungle. The tracker
Lead the way. We hoped he would find the gorillas.
Another man with a machete followed him and chopped
The vines that had grown since yesterday. One more man
Carried and old rifle, to deter poachers perhaps, or maybe
To shoot one of us if we got out of line and tried to make
Friends with the Silverback. We hiked five hours,
And then, there they were—
Eating leaves, resting among the trees and snacking
On celery roots, the Silverback in the middle,
And the babies sliding down his spine
In their misty green playground.
He let them jump on his head and yank his hair.
There were no bullies in the troop.

One of the little males grabbed your camera and played
With it for a while. We had been taught gorilla etiquette:
Sit quietly on the ground. Do not stare or show your teeth.
Turn your knuckles under, hiding your claws. Make yourself
Small. Our brothers and sisters from eons ago put up with us,
And the little guy gave you your camera back.
Decades have passed and the gorillas survived,
Eating bamboo shoots in peace, free among the leaves
While the humans squandered each other's lives.
The Silverback will have passed on by now, and the little male
Must have taken his place.
His days will end soon too, as will ours.
You, an old silverback, and I, an elder still
Able to help out with the babies, will not forget
What we witnessed among our patient hosts:
Make yourself small and live in peace.

Dear Rose Anna:
The Poet Celebrates Herself

I've been lucky.
I was born in the Ozarks with a caul over my head.
Everybody back there knows that a girl born with a caul
Will be clairvoyant. That's a big word for the Ozarks,
But everyone knows what it means. I always felt
Just a little special, like I carried a secret locket in my heart.
My name was another lucky gift, a beautiful name
That I never resented or wanted to change.
Other people changed it for me.
Grandpa always called me Rosie, but that was okay
Because he bought me more fireworks than any girl could
Dream of and let me shoot them off all by myself all day
And all night every Fourth of July, and I never blew my
Fingers off. That was another stroke of luck.

My husband just calls me Rose, and that's all right too,
Because he grew up in Japan where a person's middle name
Is private. When my family finally got to California,
Everybody there was in such a hurry, they couldn't even be
Bothered to say their whole first name when they met you.
They called themselves Mo and Tori and Dru, half of a name,
And you never learned what their last name was,
Like their parents and grandparents didn't matter at all.
They matter to me. If Rose Anna, my great grandmother,
Hadn't immigrated, I wouldn't be Rose Anna at all,
And neither would the other three Rose Annas named after her.

They're all dead now, and I'm getting closer.
I think about it every day.
When my dad was the age I am now, he had been dead
For three years, but my mother had twelve more years to live.
Where am I on this scale? I don't know.

I'm not really that clairvoyant.
I do know I'm lucky to have a son who still loves me
And a husband who's stuck by me for sixty plus years.
I don't want to get greedy. I'm no Louise Gluck
Who won every poetry prize on Earth, but it would
Be nice if I could be as lucky as Emily Dickinson
Or Gerard Manley Hopkins, who both had somebody
Who cared about them even after they were dead,
And knew how to send their poems out into the world.
That would really be lucky if my poetry still floated around
For a while after I'm off with all the other Rose Annas.

The Grace of Ghosts

As I stretch through my morning yoga,
My sister Margaret reaches out to me.
She died five years ago, but somehow
Grief's resurgence has a timeline of its own.
Tears start flowing as I place my legs into
Child's Pose, a bit awkward, as my husband
Is also stretching in the same room. He's
Concentrating and doesn't notice. My nose
Starts running onto the yoga mat, and I feel the
Urge to keep this event a secret between
Margaret and me. Is that how it is with ghosts?
Are they secrets that belong to each of us?
They have always been present, whispering
In the mists, fleeing through our dreams,
Echoing strangely in the tide as the foam rolls
Up the sand, flickering in a butterfly's blue wing
Or scenting our space with roses from long ago.
We have read *Macbeth,* seen that terrifying play and
Learned that murder, cruelty and greed do not
Generate serenity in the next world. To free ourselves
From fear, we create silly movies and cartoon characters
About ghosts, but we remain conflicted whether these
Beings are good or evil. Aren't they just like us?
Some souls glitter with glory; others carry the burden
Of rage and shame. I stretch my hands high into the sky
And touch my sister's soft fingers, thanking her
For all that she was and is.

Sonnet Counterpoint

Sometimes a circle is a fairy ring,
Sometimes a yin and yang, sometimes a dome
Of healing, sometimes a cyclone of pain.
The seasons cycle with pine wind and chill;
Then manzanita bells ring in the rain,
And blossoms blow in the sun's golden will
As spring surges up with green once again.
Then geese fly above and our spirits soar
Till mud and shame sink our souls at the core,
So we trudge on or skip or run, swallow
Our pride or glory in the sun. Up, down
And all around, so dizzy as we go
Some dropping trails of breadcrumbs behind,
Some casting their kite in the western wind.

About the Author

Rose Anna Higashi was born in Joplin Missouri and, during childhood, lived in various locations in Kansas and the Pacific Northwest with her parents, brother, and sister while her father, Patrick Murdock, completed his Ph.D. in History from Washington State University in Pullman, and her mother, Betty Murdock, earned her Ph.D. in Speech from the University of Missouri in Columbia.

After the family settled in California when Rose Anna was twelve, Patrick and Betty both had long careers in public education, Patrick as a history professor and Betty as a school speech pathologist. Rose Anna spent the majority of her adult life in Northern California where she completed her BA and MA degrees in English Literature, *suma cum laude,* from San Jose State University.

When she was eighteen, Rose Anna married Wayne Higashi, a friend from high school whom she met at the age of fifteen. They are the parents of one son, David Higashi. Wayne and Rose Anna have been married for more than sixty years and have traveled together extensively throughout the world. Rose Anna taught English at San Jose State University and San Jose City College and volunteered to be a founding faculty member when a new California Community College, Evergreen Valley College, was constructed in San Jose in 1975 to accommodate the growth of Silicon Valley and the arrival in San Jose of thousands of refugees from Vietnam.

At Evergreen Valley College, Rose Anna founded the Spring Poetry Festival and the literary magazine *Leaf by Leaf.* In addition to English Composition, she taught Poetry, Creative Writing, Survey of English Literature, Shakespeare, Women in Literature, Asian and Asian American Literature, and Japanese Literature.

She developed the Japanese Literature course herself and introduced it into the curriculum, the first Japanese Literature class to be offered at a California community college. Rose Anna studied Japanese Language and Japanese Literature in greater depth during a sabbatical year at Stanford University.

Rose Anna's Publications include the poetry collections *Rose Anna's Gift* and *Blue Wings* (Paulist Press). She is also the author of a novel, *The Learning Wars*.

For the past fourteen years, she has written a haiku every day. She was a finalist in the Filoli Haiku Contest and was recently nominated by the Editors of Poets Online for the Pushcart Prize. Her poetry appears in *Poets Online, Verse-Virtual, Spillwords, The Ekphrastic Review, The Agape Review, America Media, The Avocet, Integrated Catholic Life, The Scarlet Dragonfly Review,* and other publications.

Rose Anna and Wayne are retired and now live in Honolulu where they continue to travel, and Rose Anna continues to write and publish poetry. She is an active member of the Union of Poets Virtual Open Mic, an international group of poets who share their poems virtually each month.

Her website, co-authored with her niece Kathleen Pedulla, hosts her monthly blog, "Tea and Travels," along with many of her haiku and lyric poems.

Website:
myteaplanner.com

www.ingramcontent.com/pod-product-compliance
Lightning Source LLC
Chambersburg PA
CBHW022011160426
43197CB00007B/383